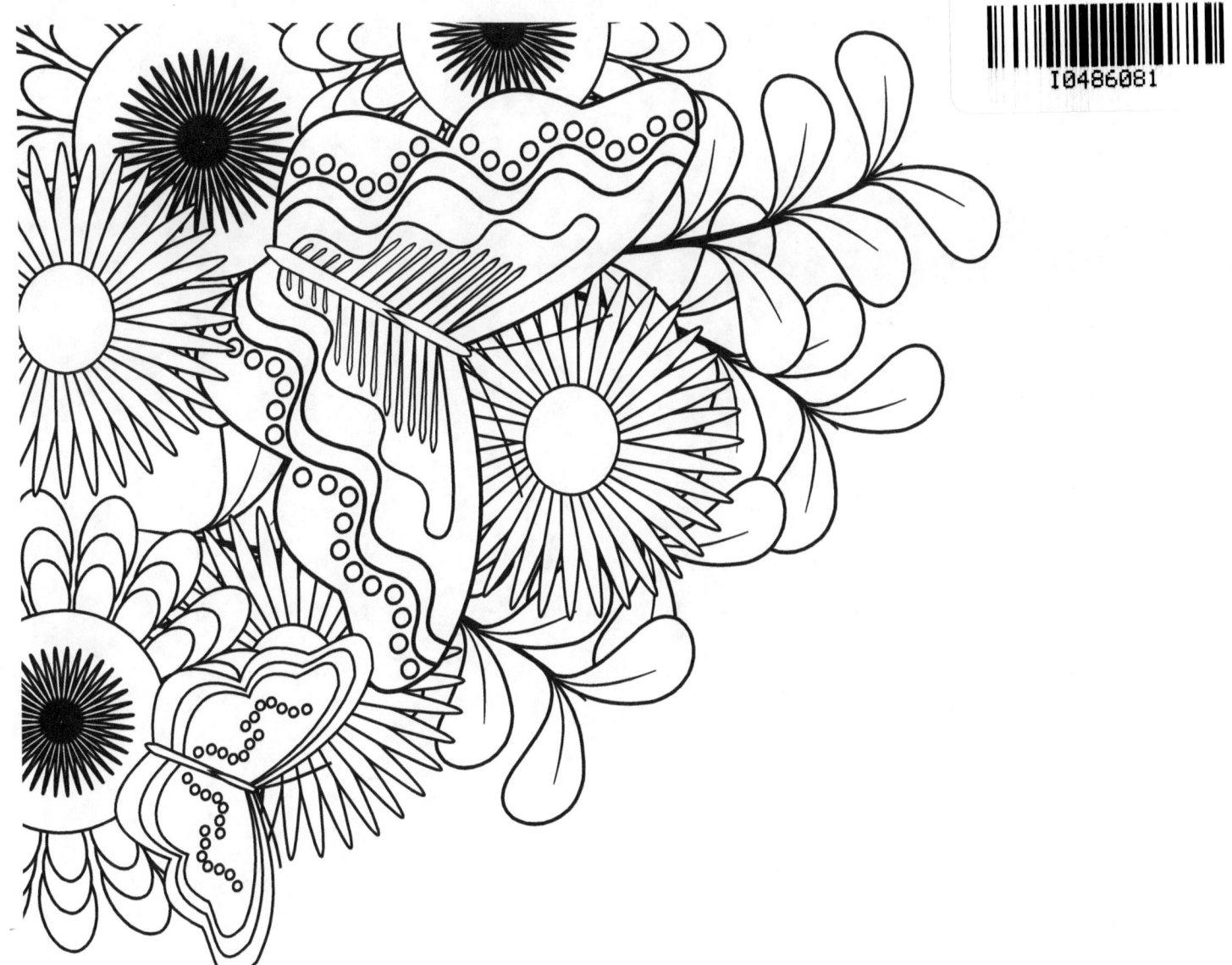

STRESS RELIEF COLORING

AN ADULT COLORING BOOK

Hey!

Thanks for your support, you beautiful person! My name is Michelle Nguyen - the one woman team behind this coloring book. Being a one woman team, I have lovingly designed every single aspect of this book, from cover to back and every pattern in between.

As a twenty- something still trying to figure her life out (and one who disappointed her parents by not becoming a doctor), I find coloring washes my worries away with every single colorful stroke. With that being said, I hope you find your worries are a little less worrisome as you delve deeper into the pages here.

Here is to staying inside the lines or out - if that's your thing!

Michelle

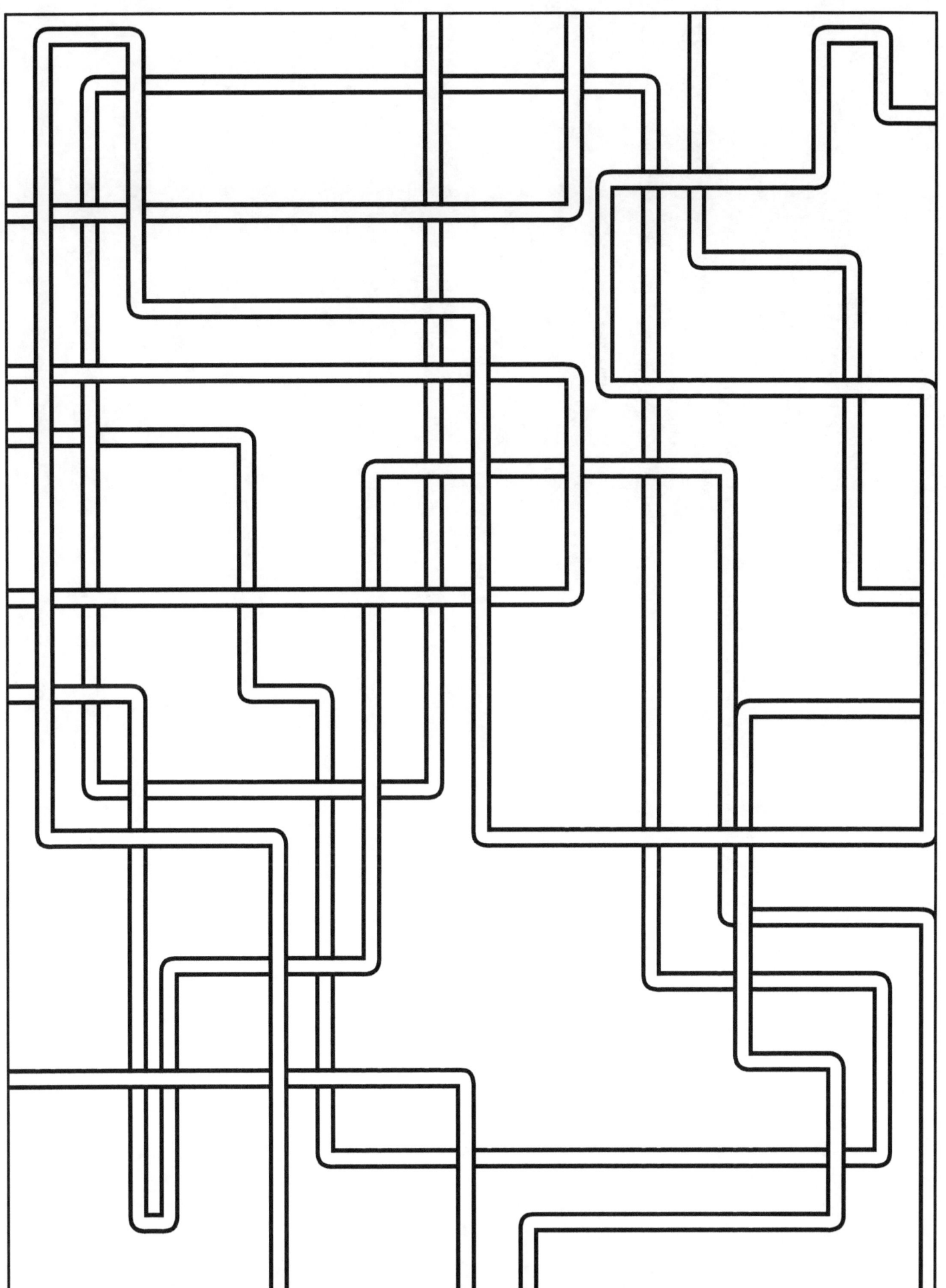

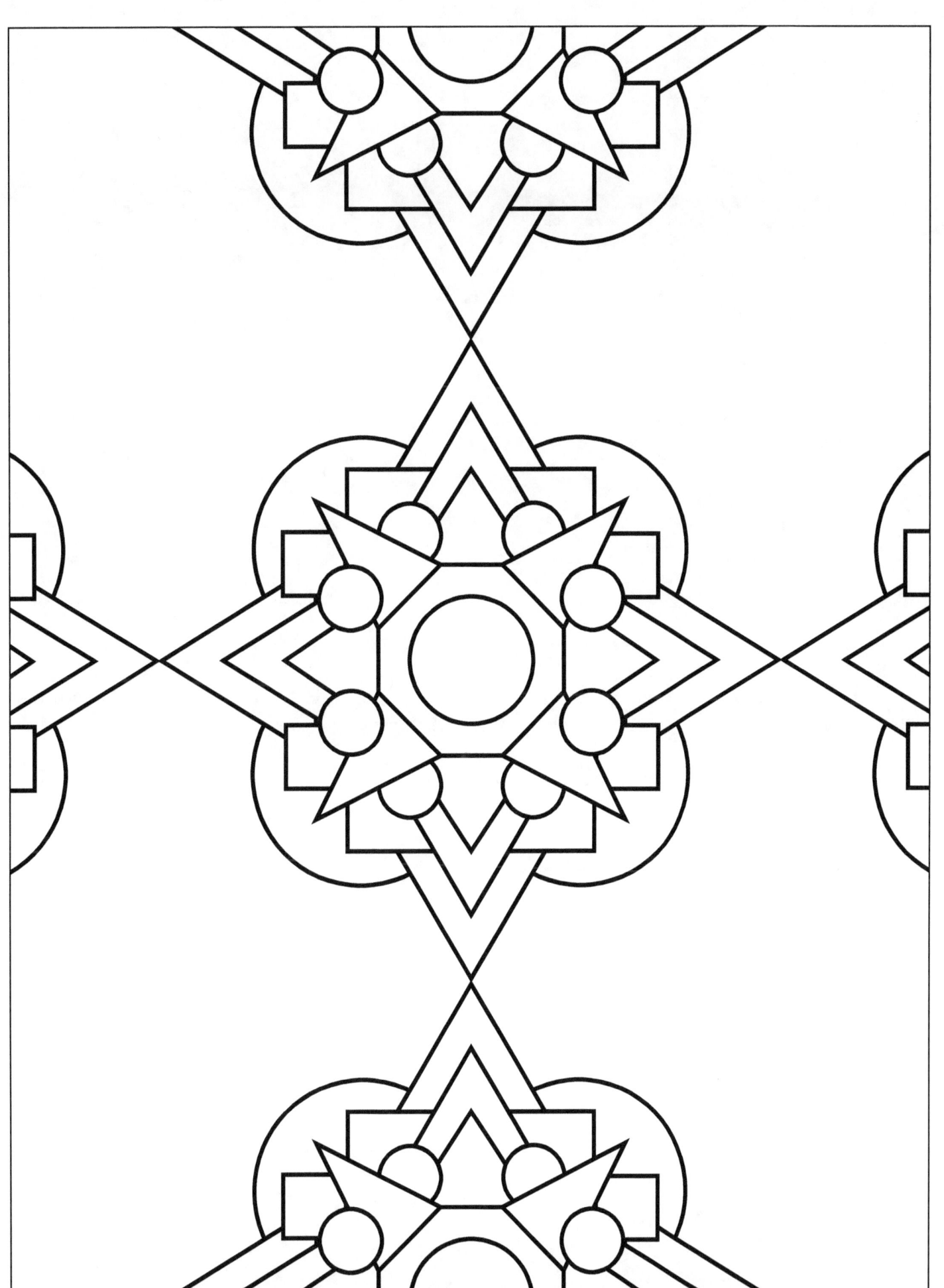

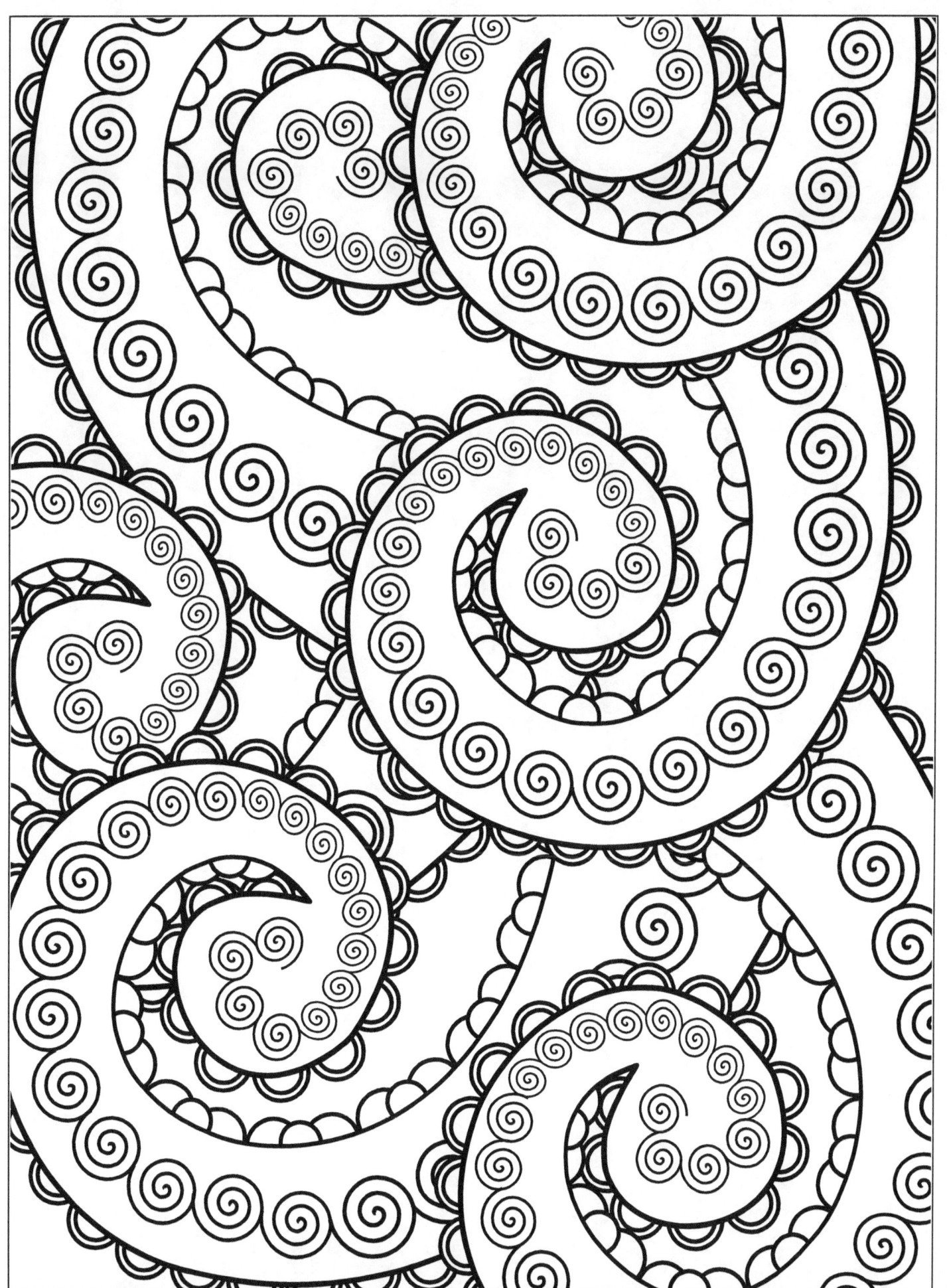

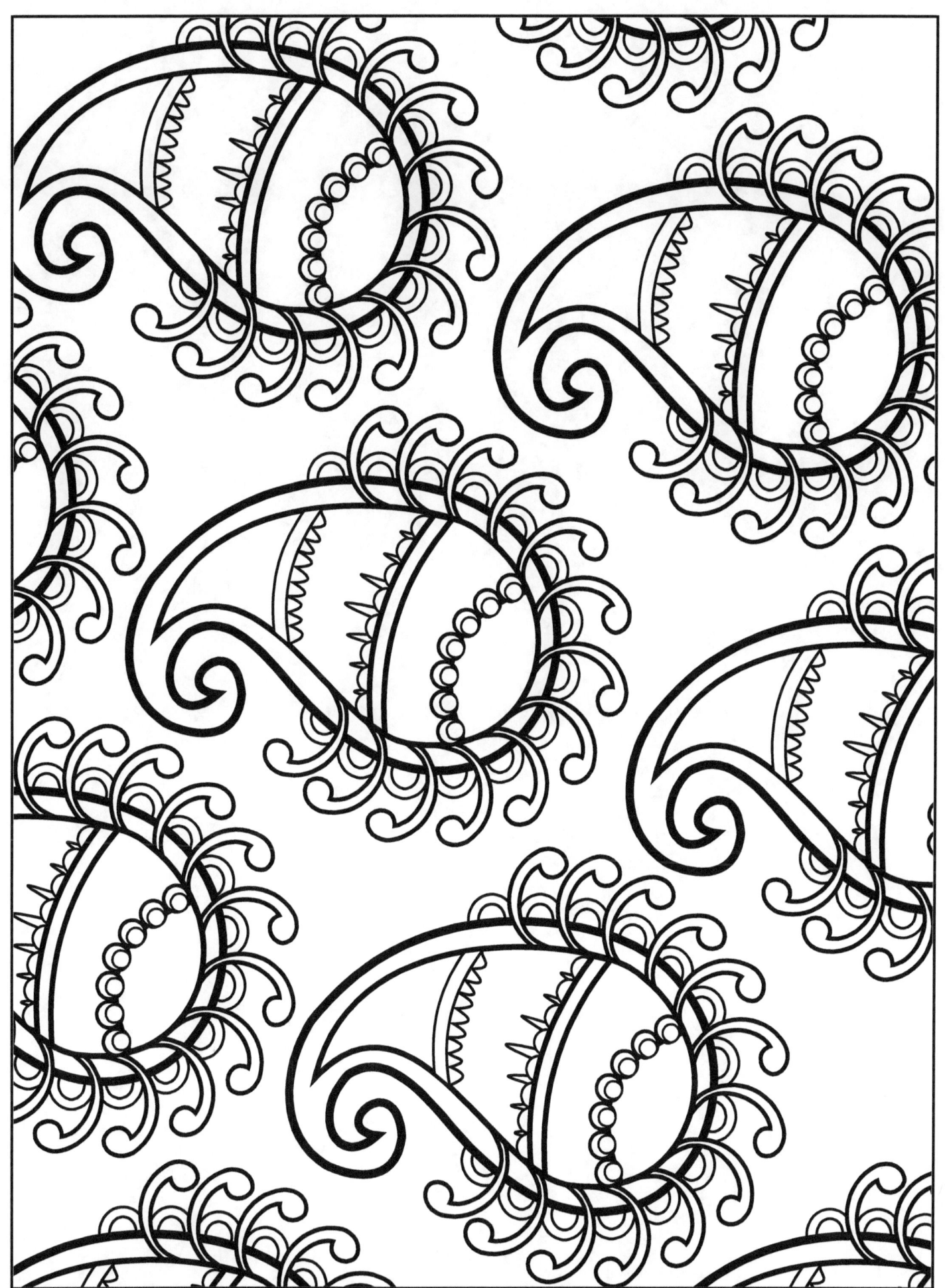

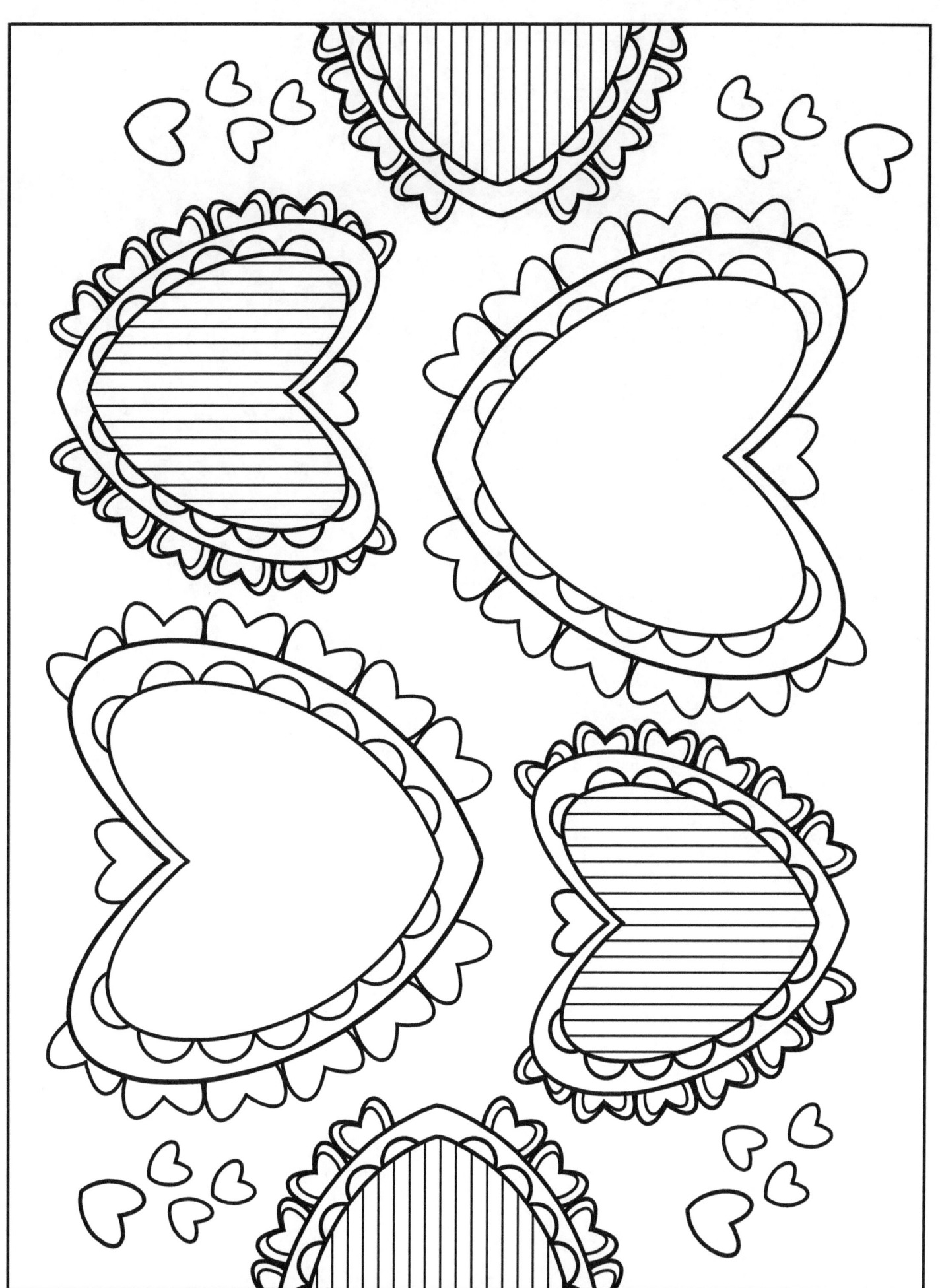

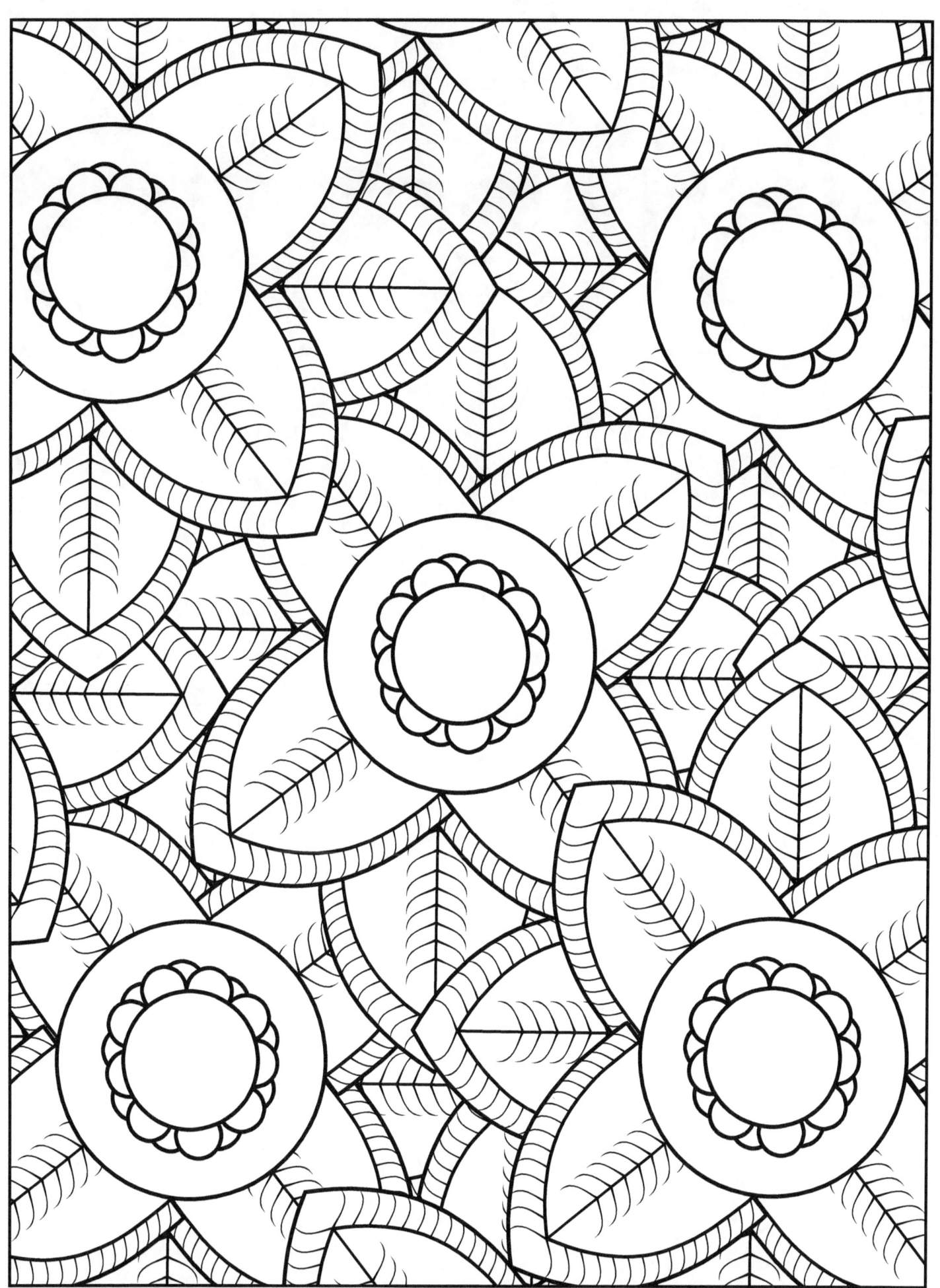

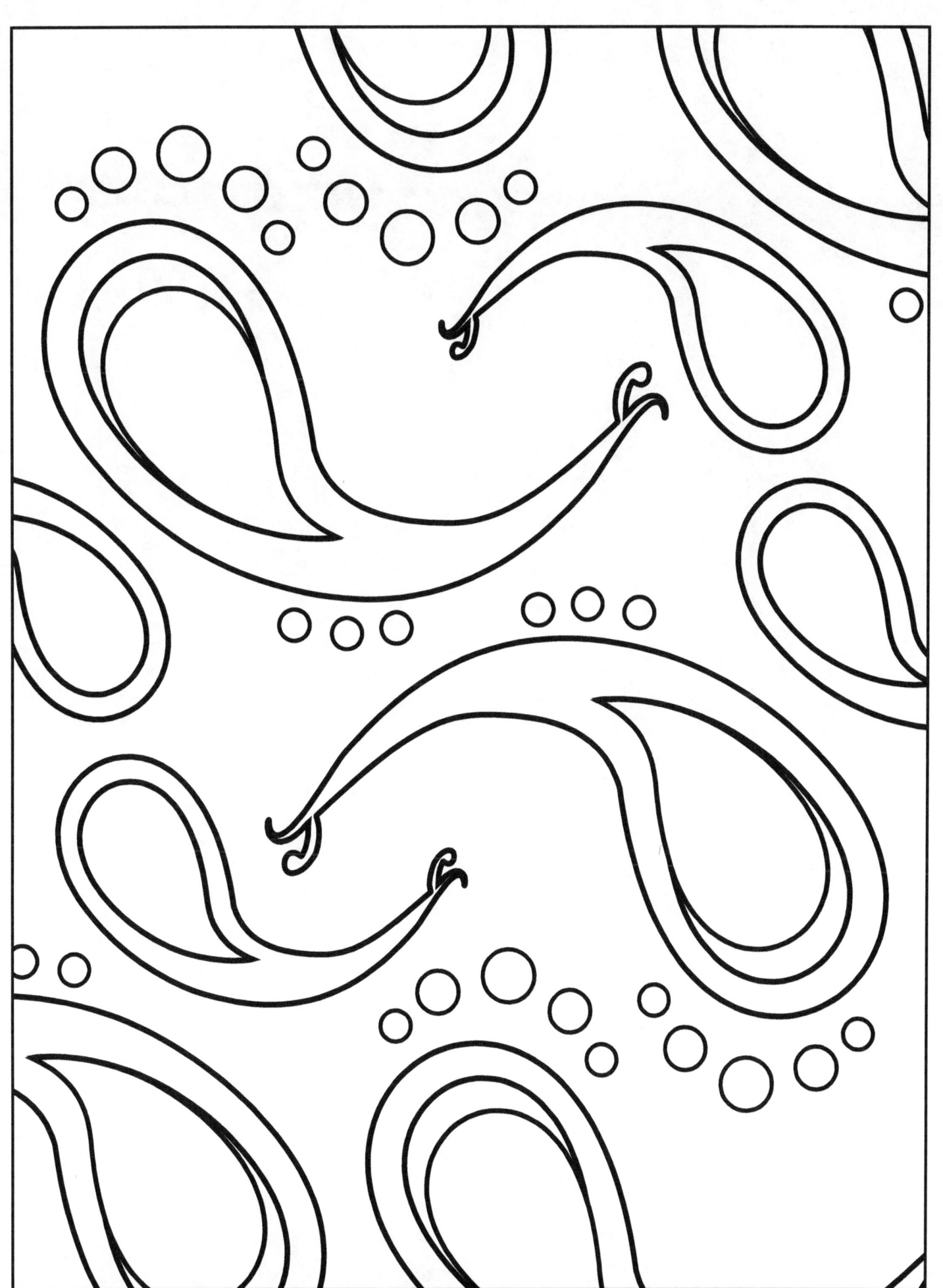

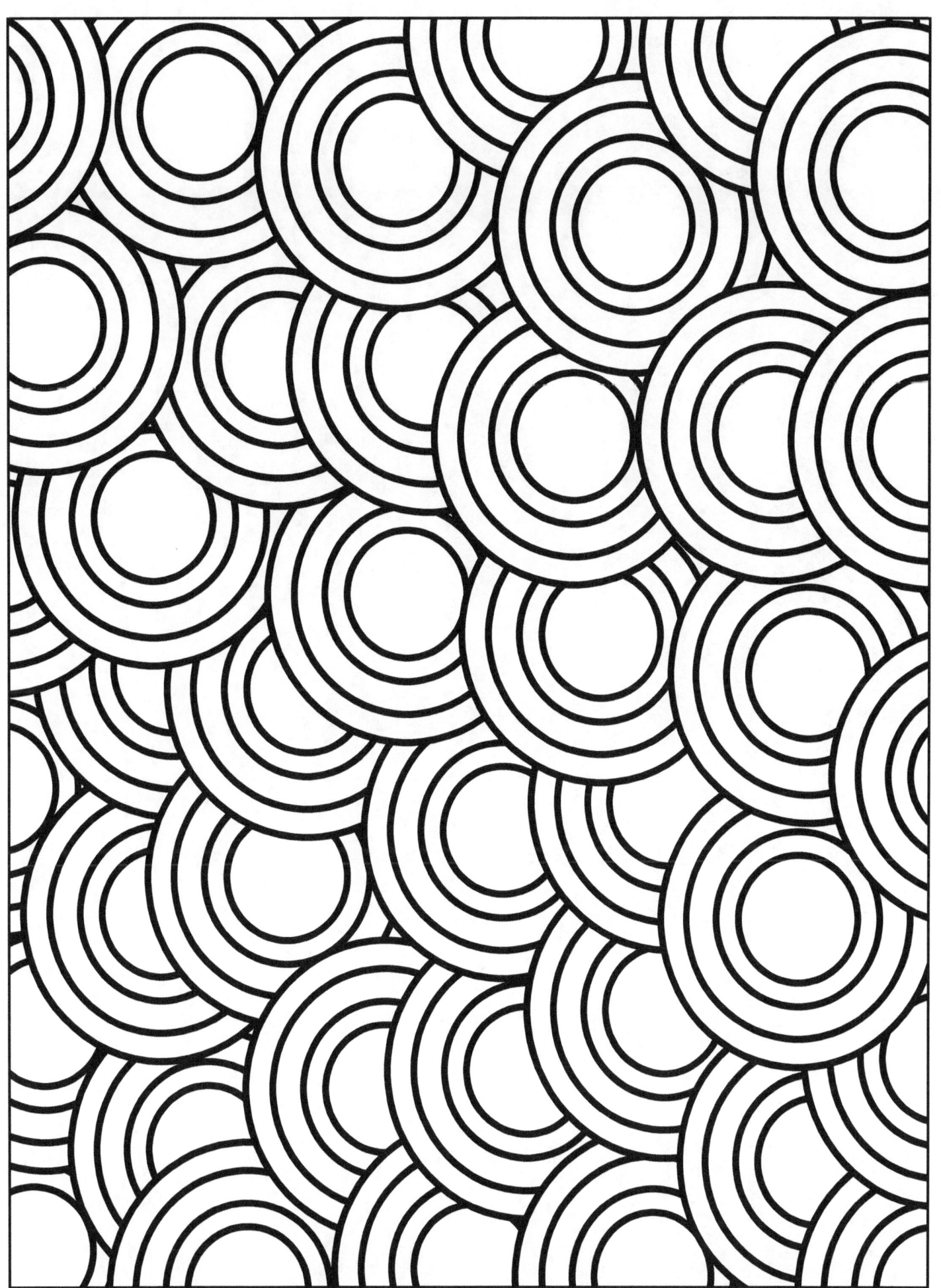

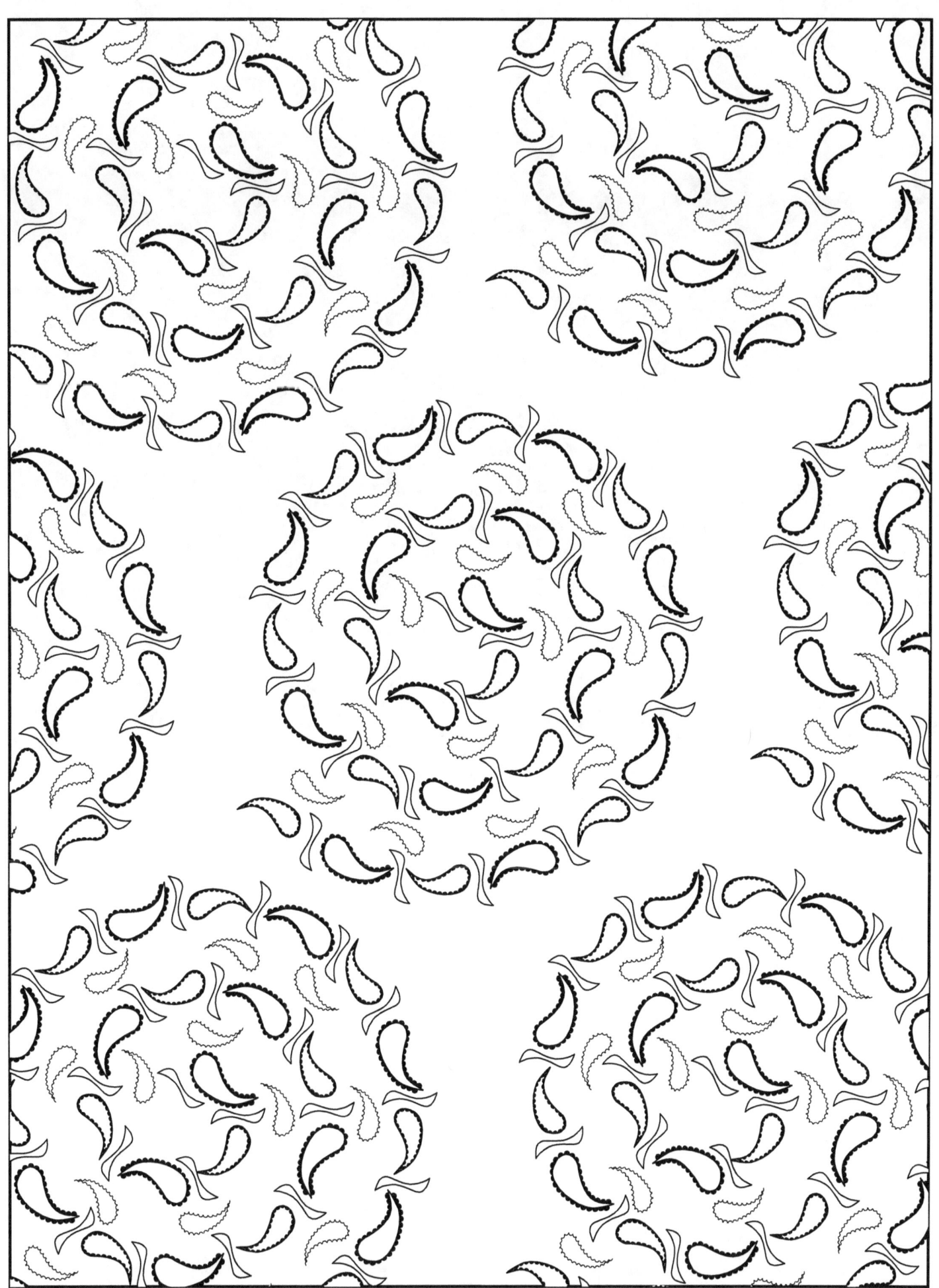

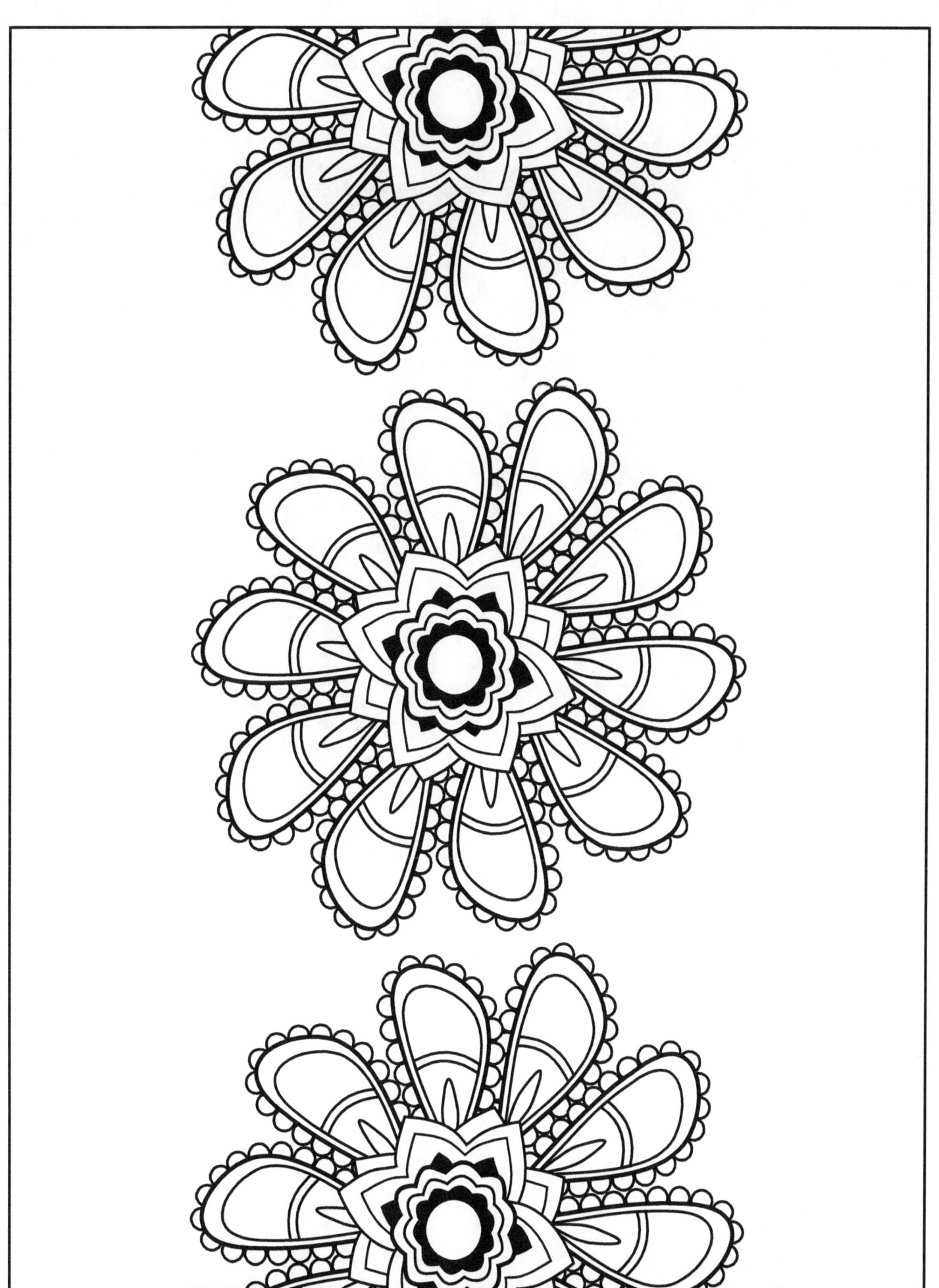

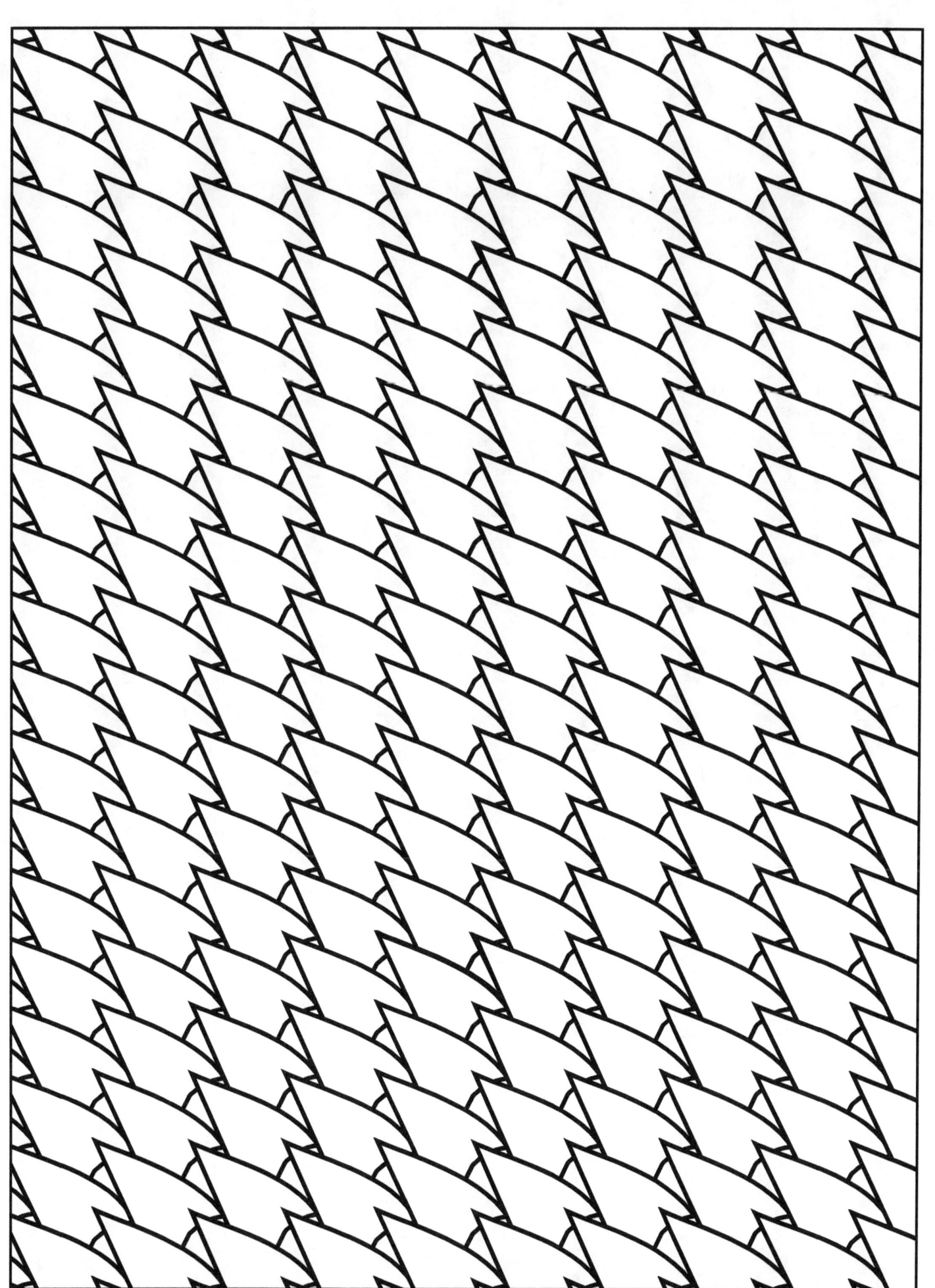

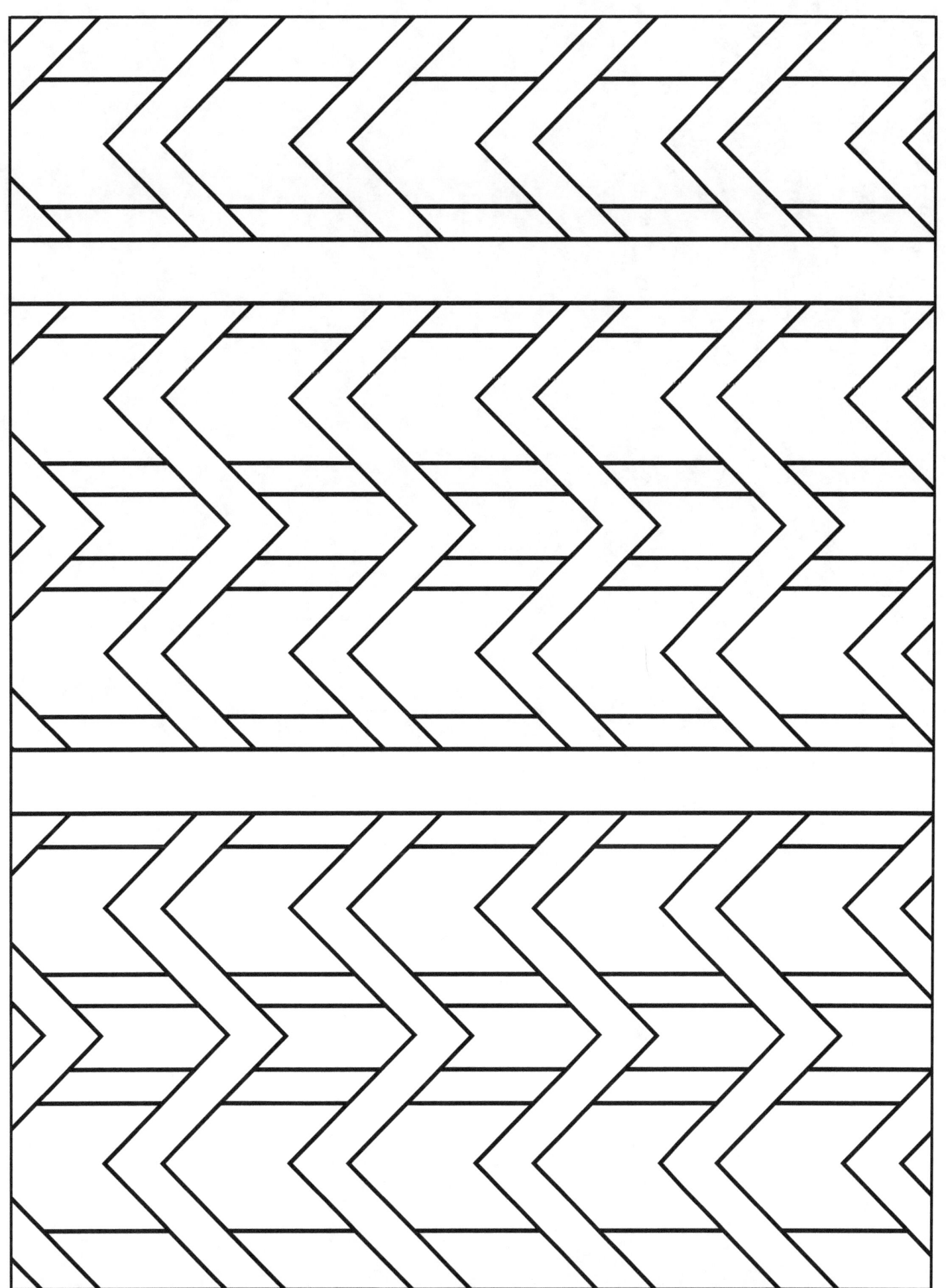

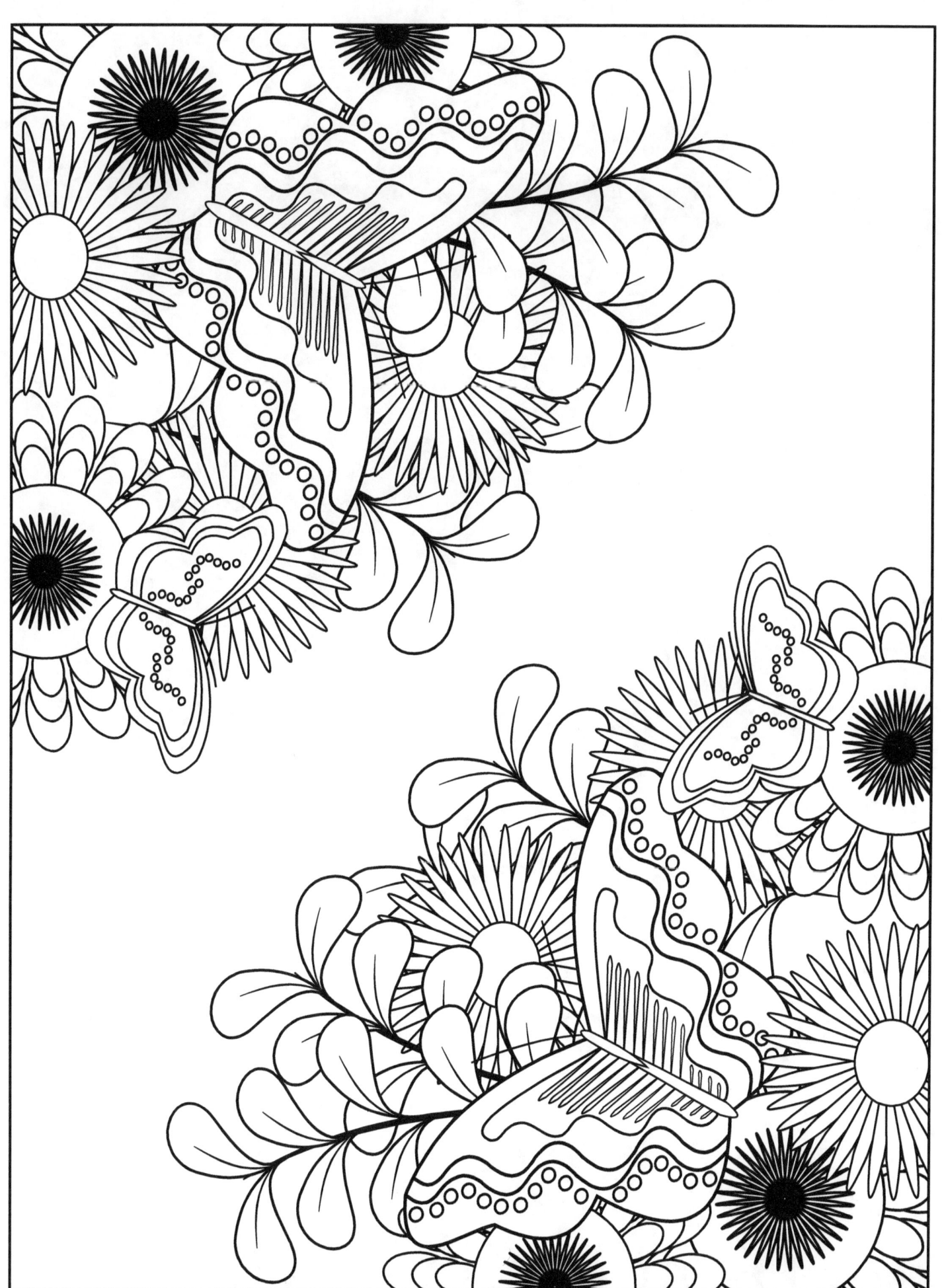

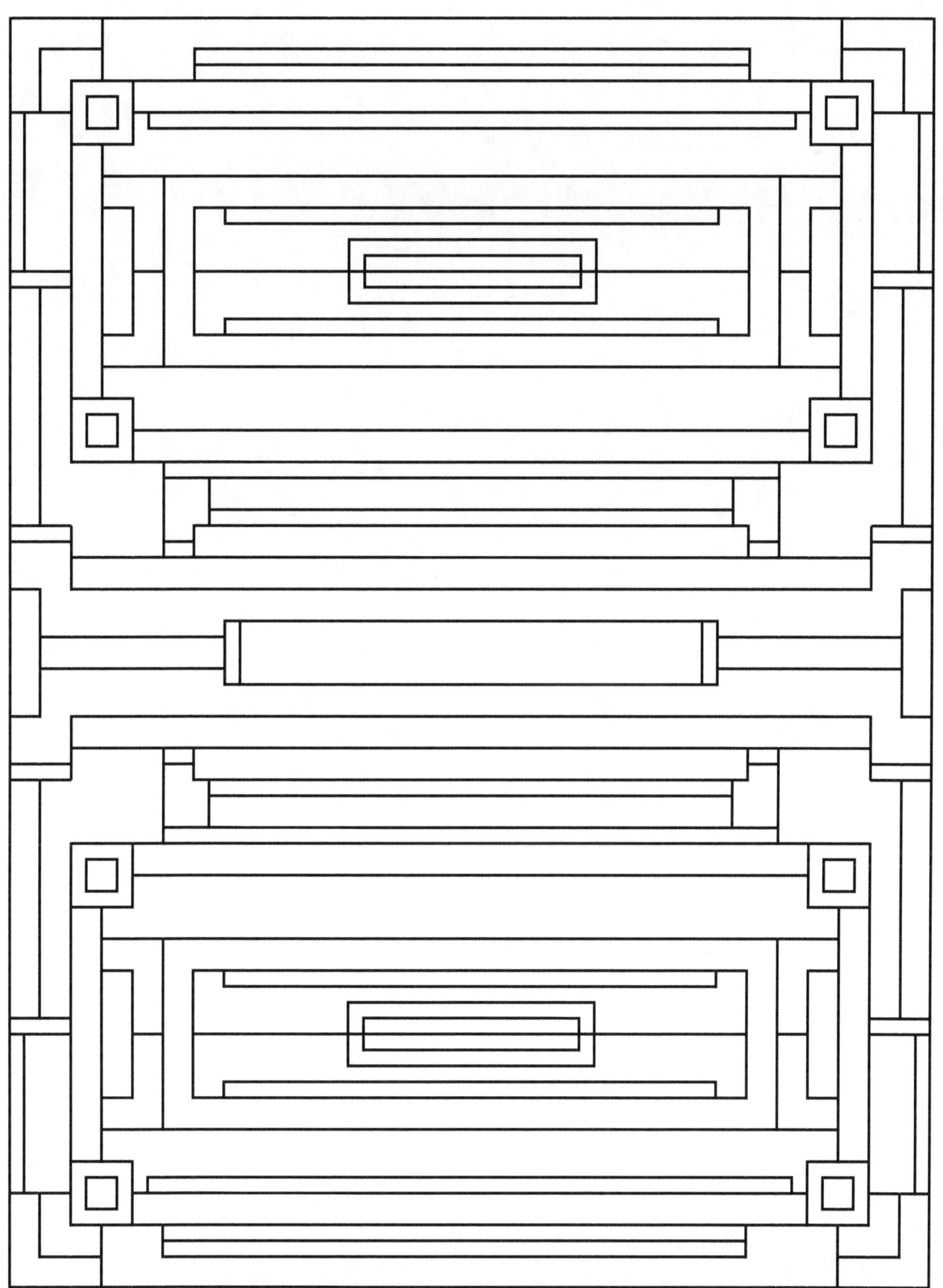

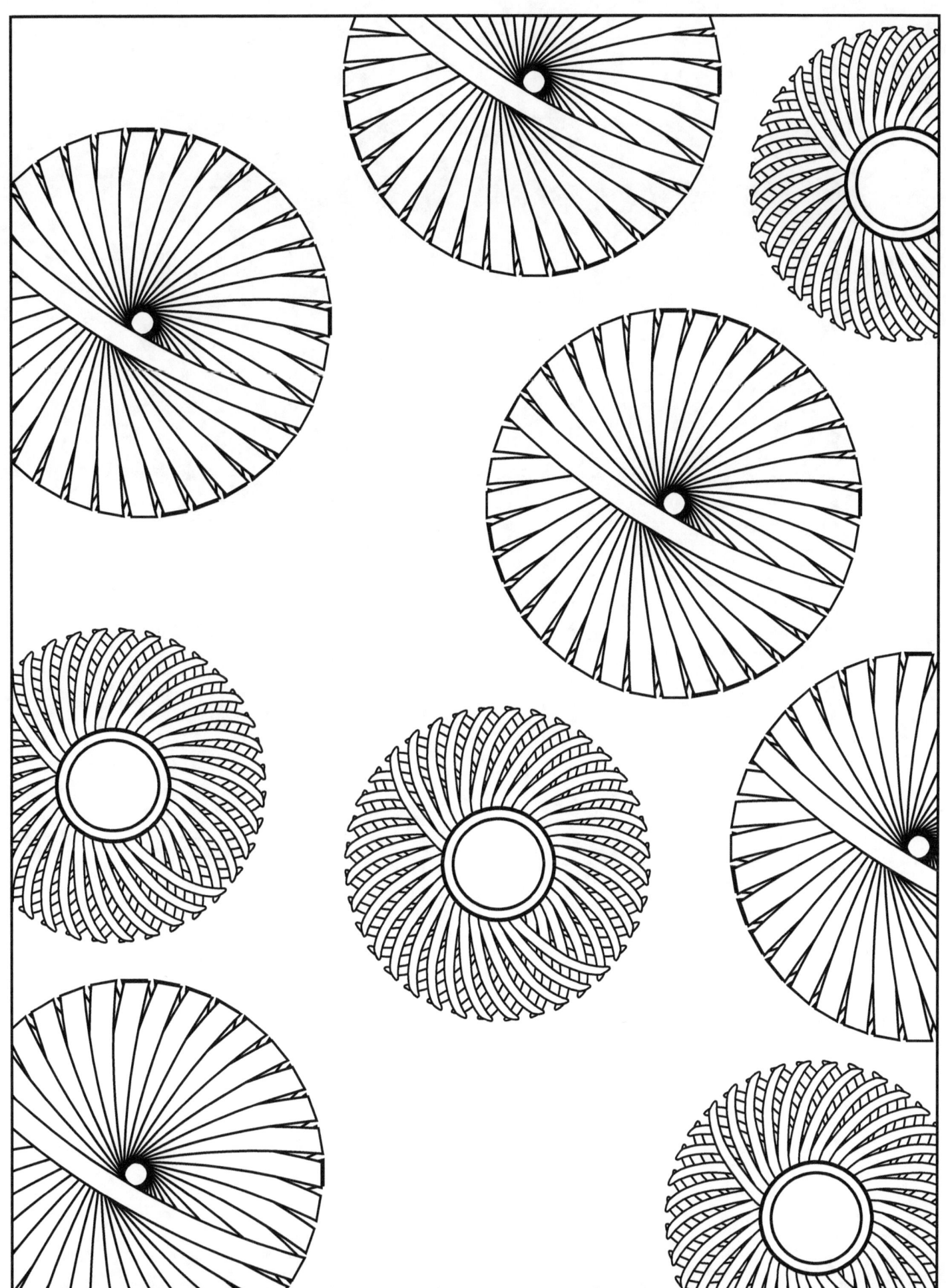

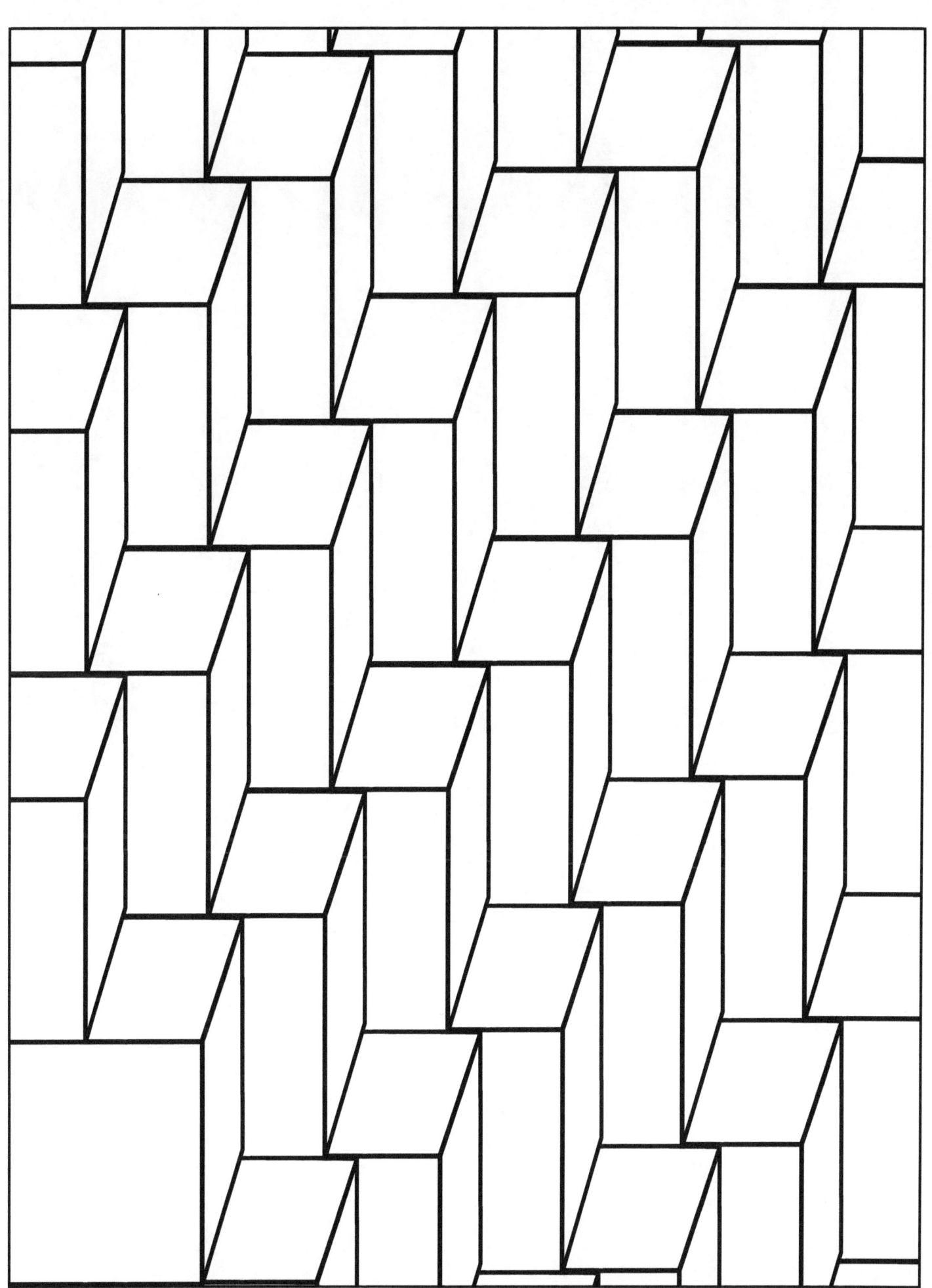

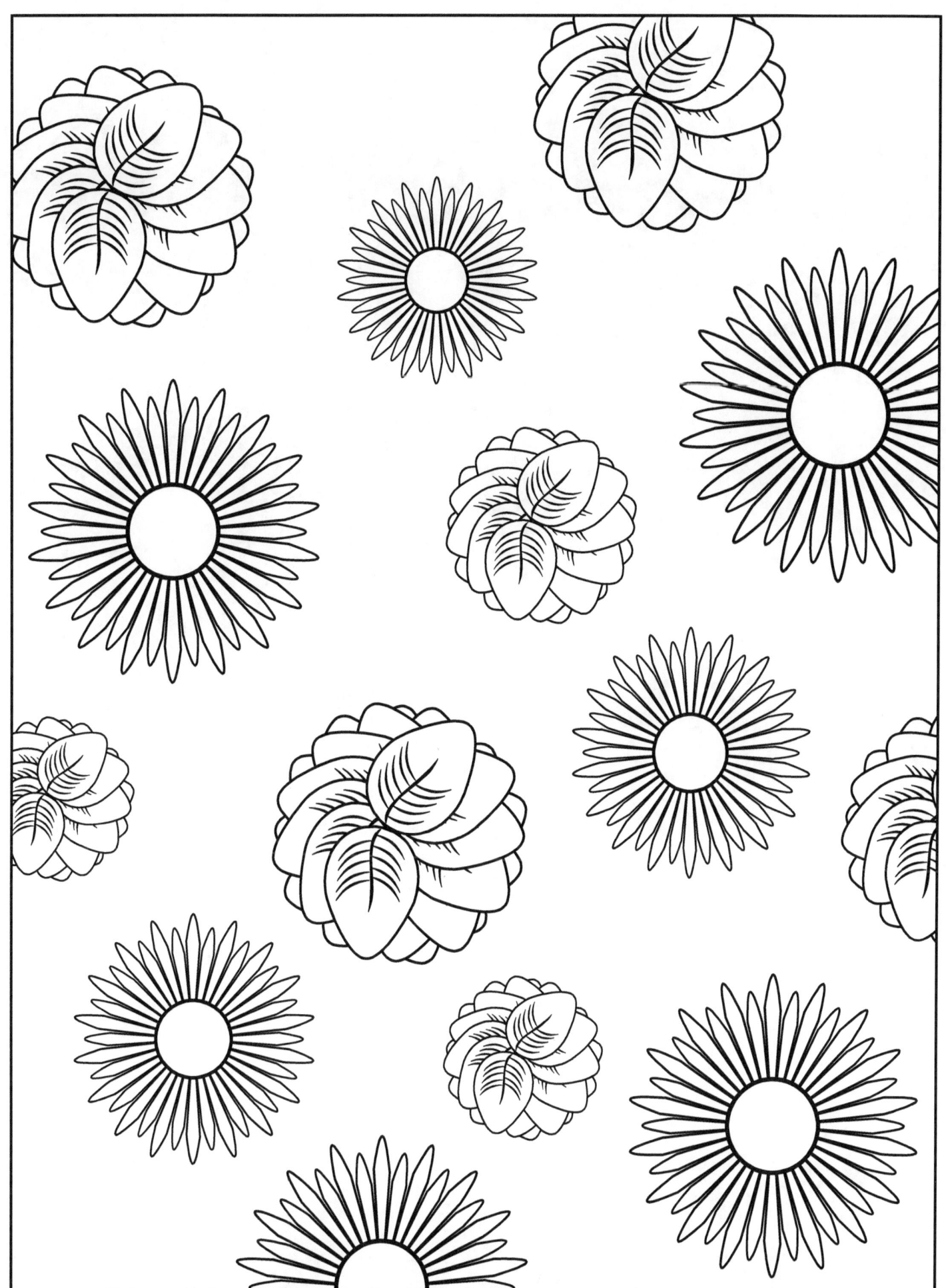

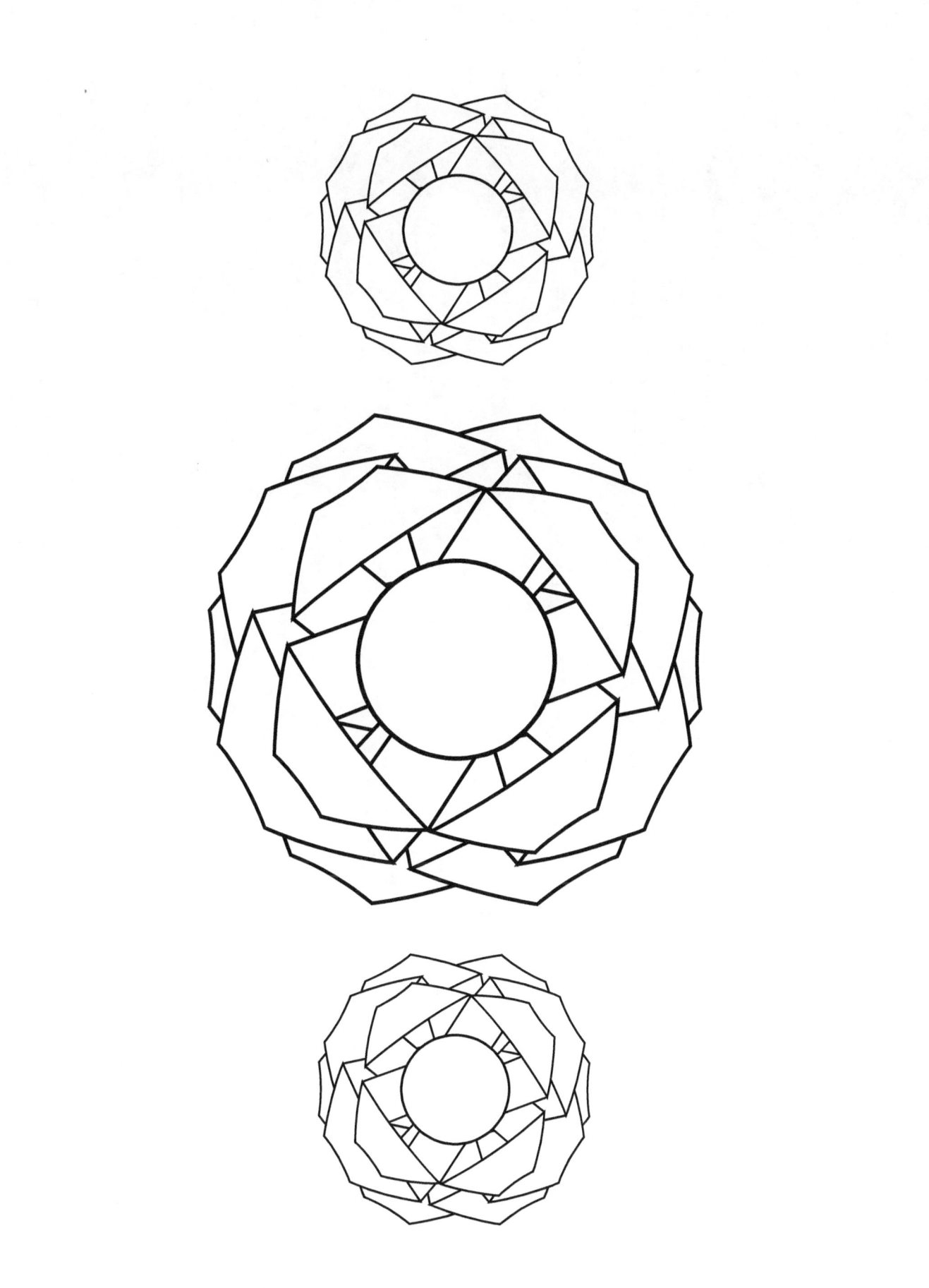

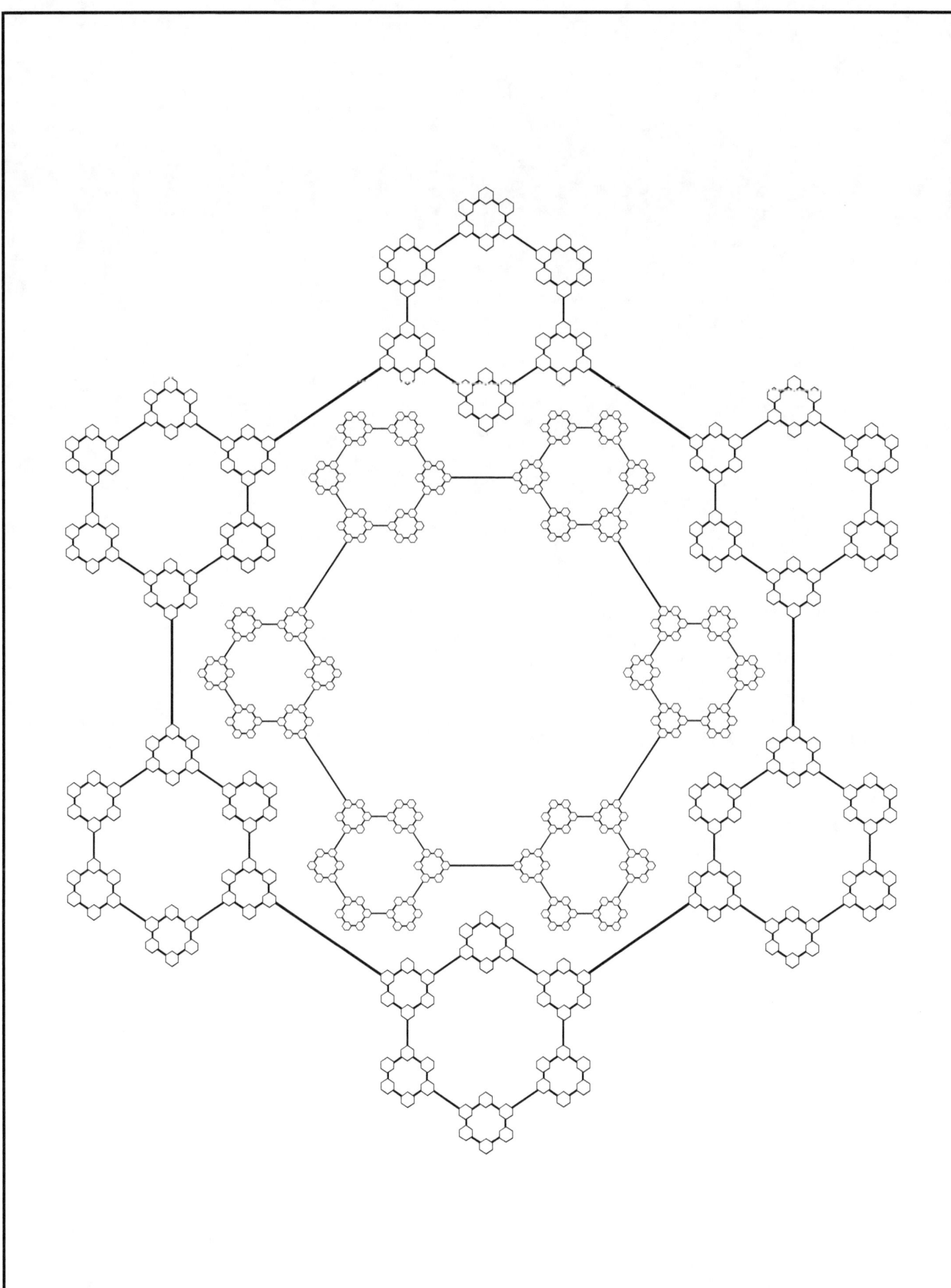

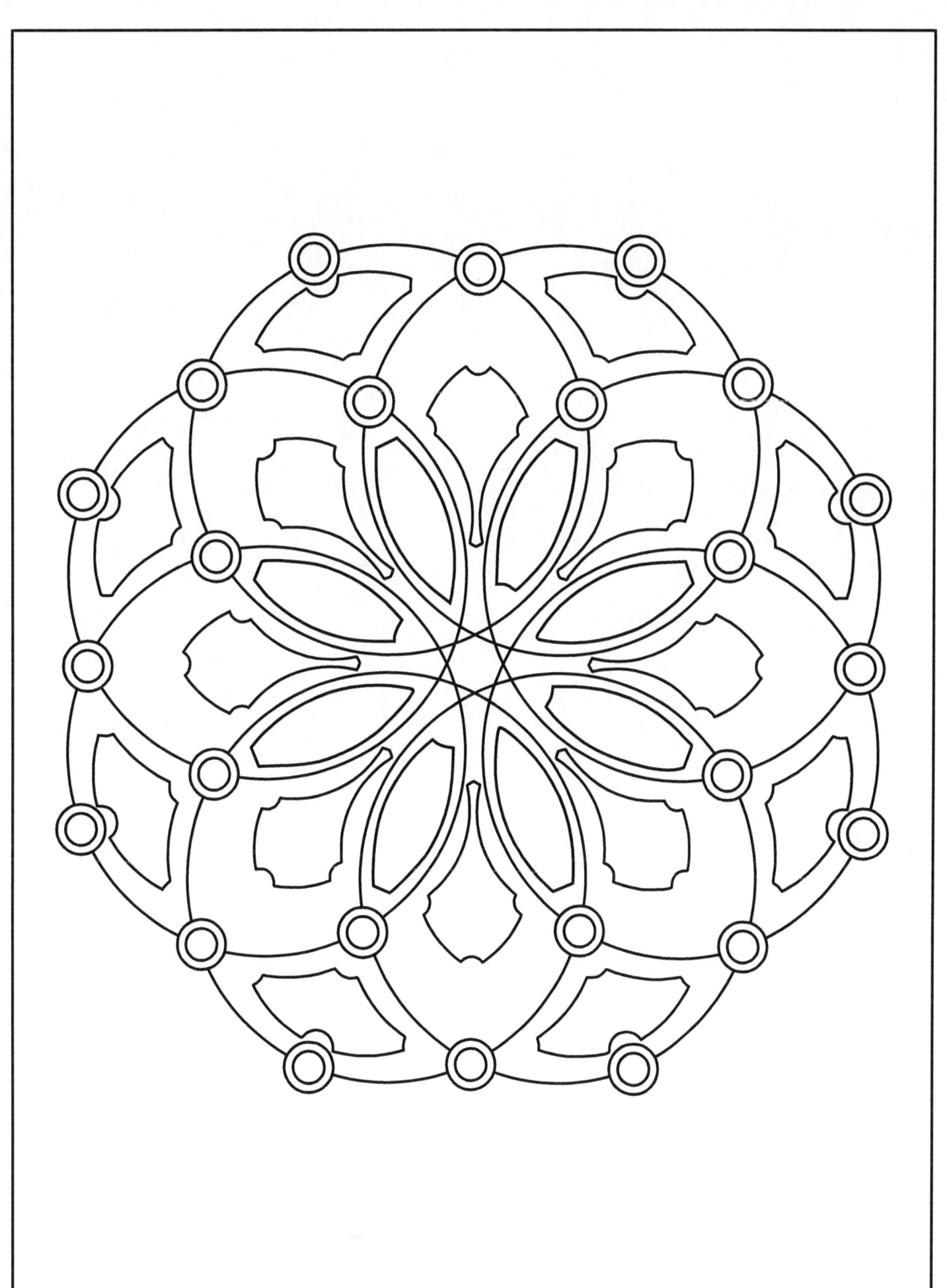

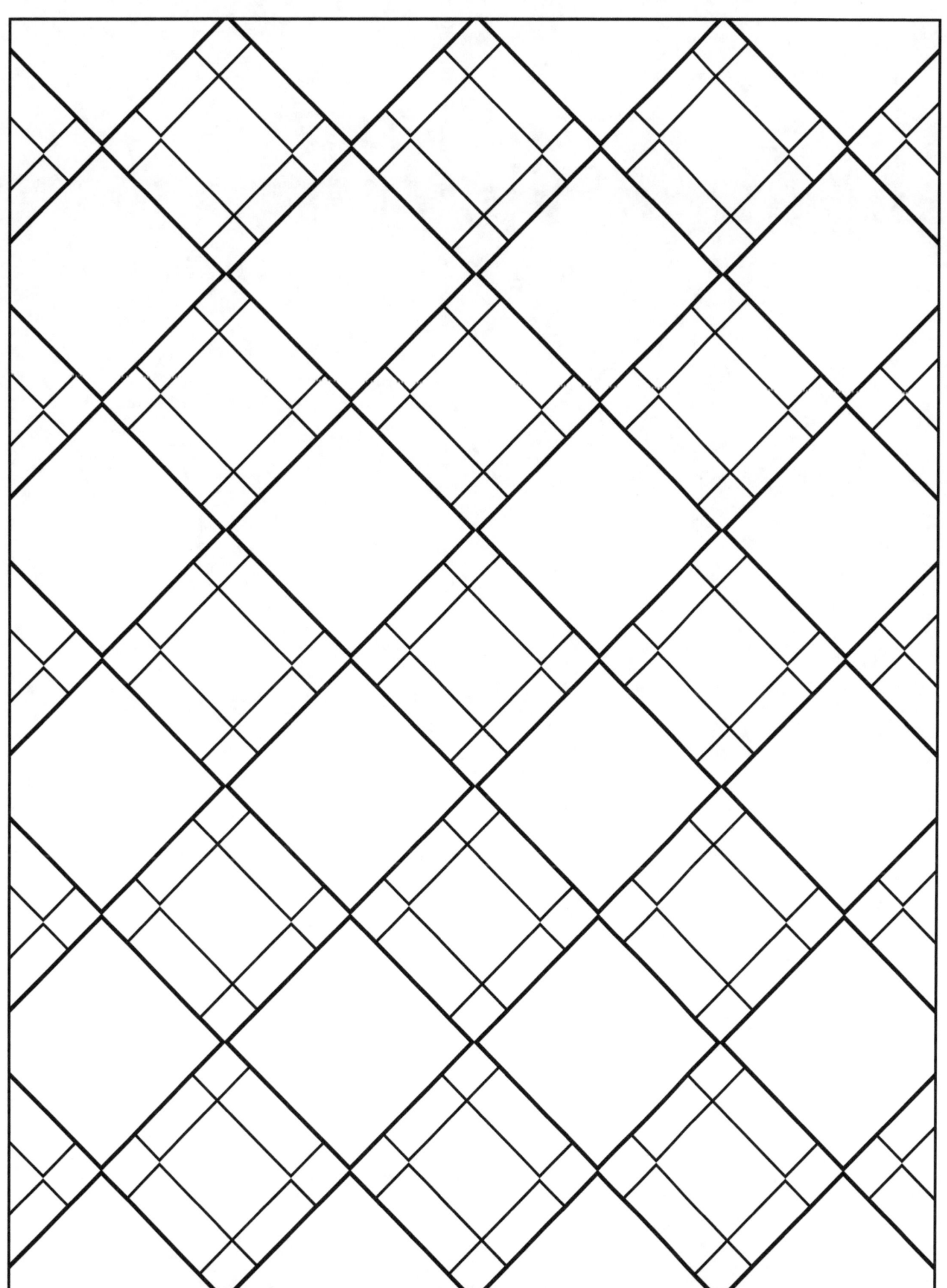

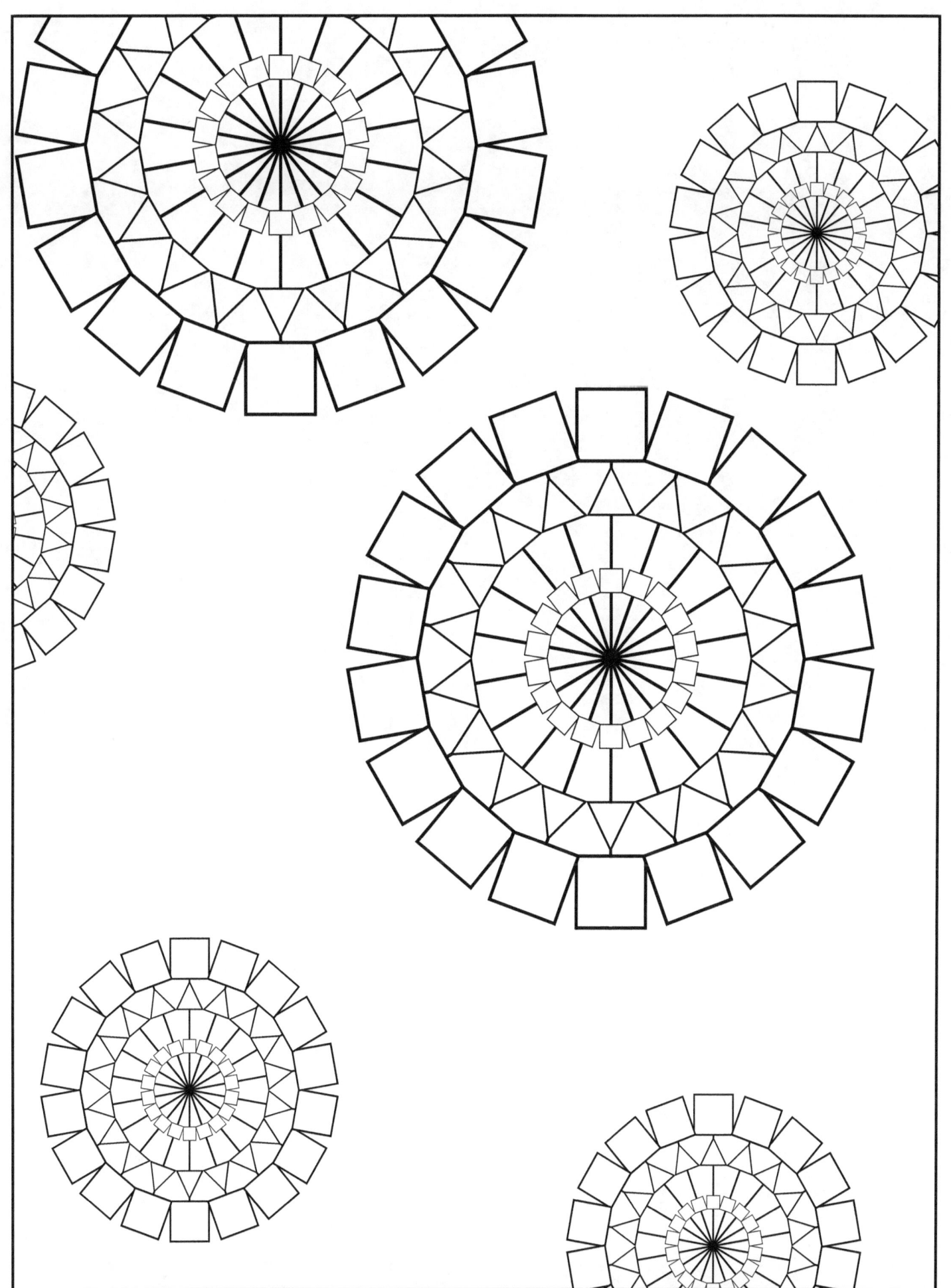

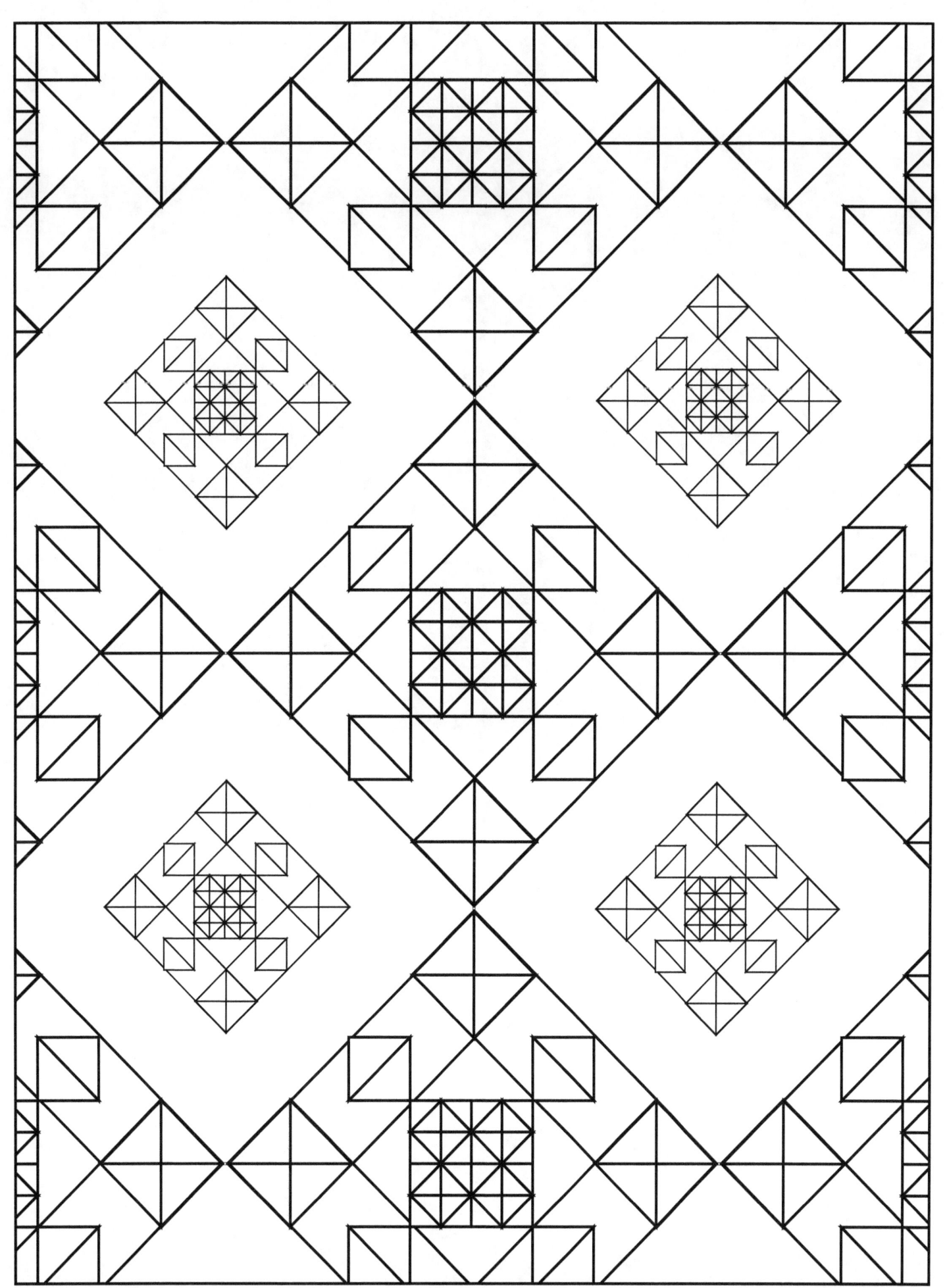

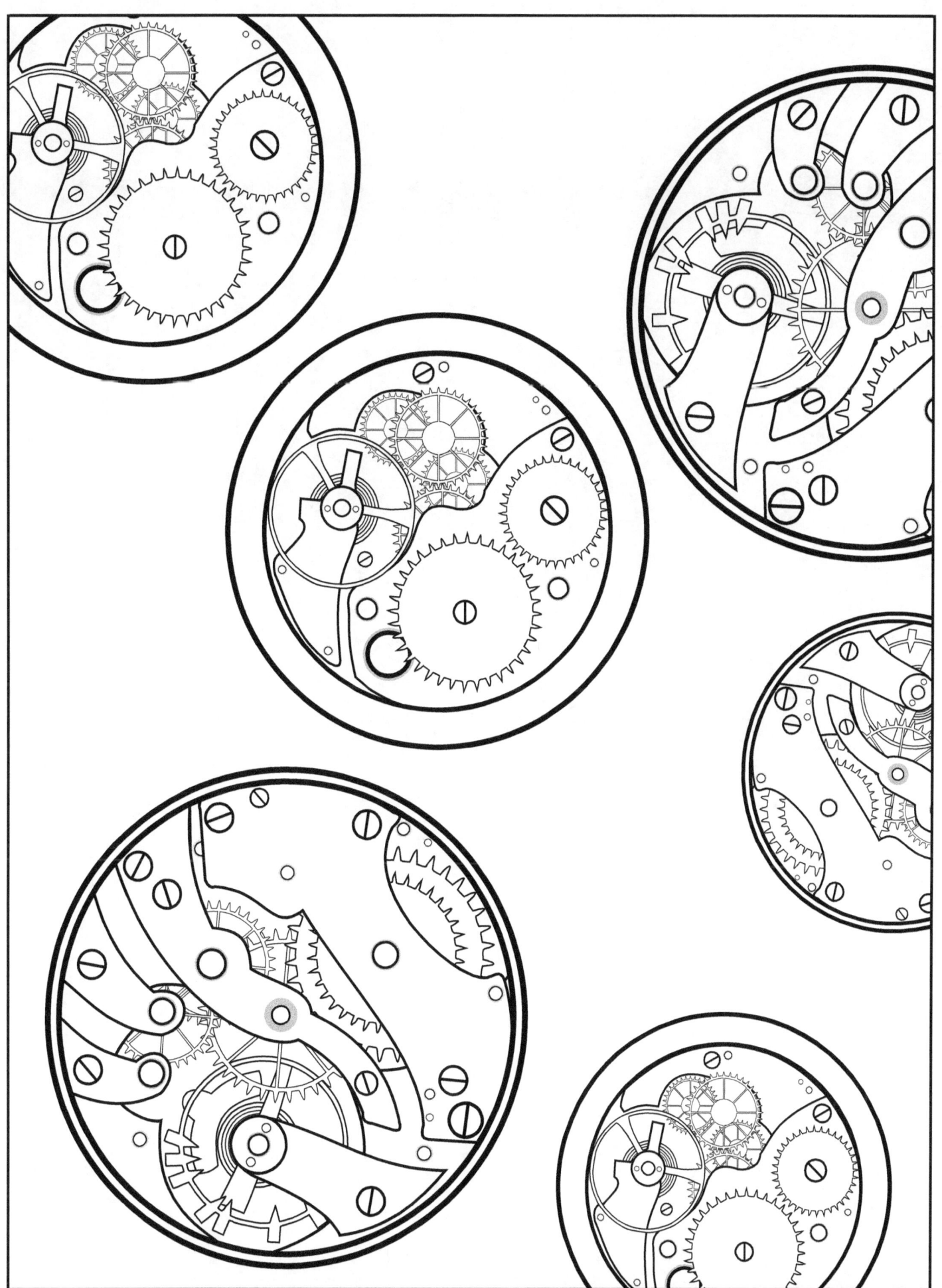

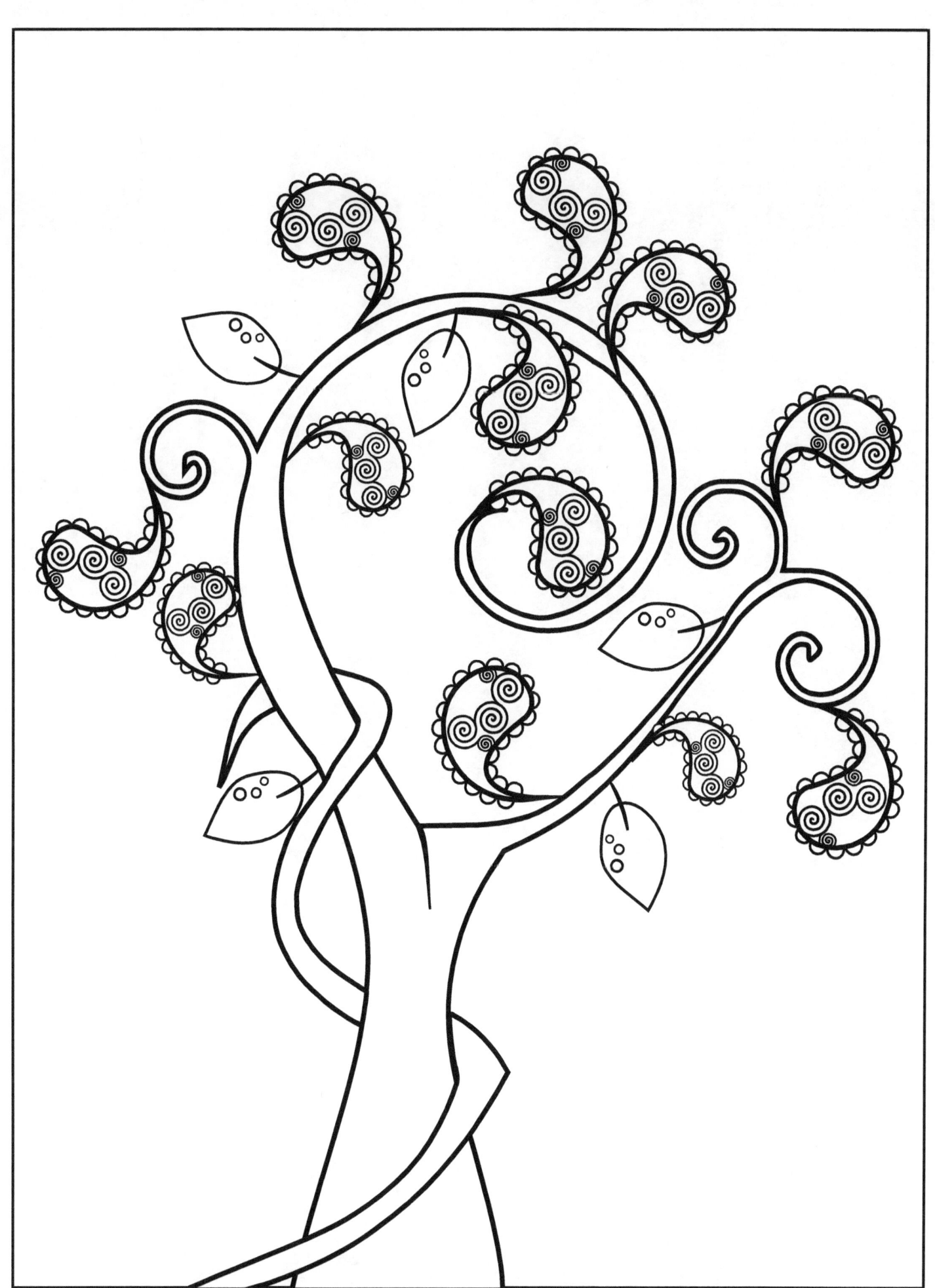

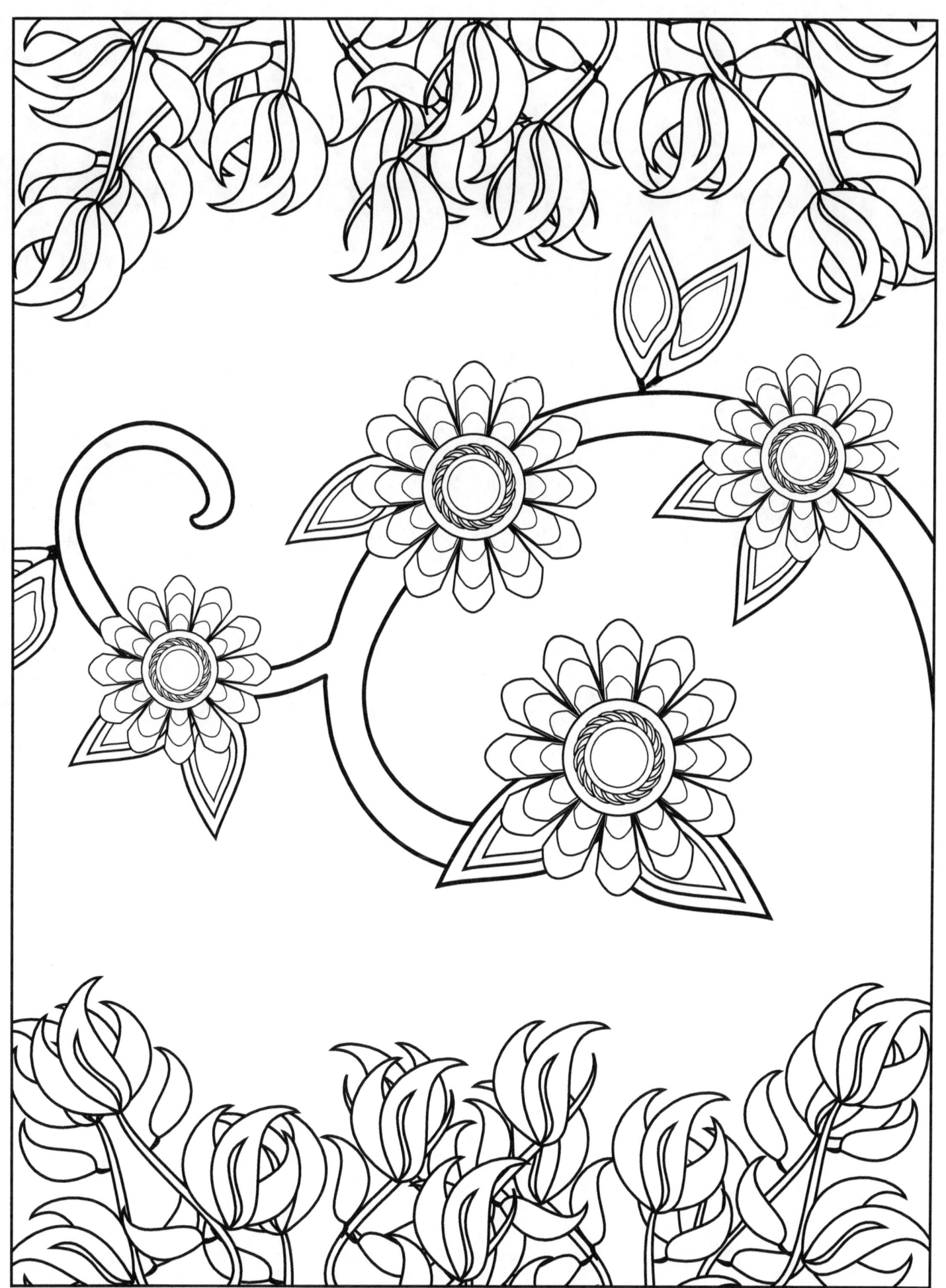

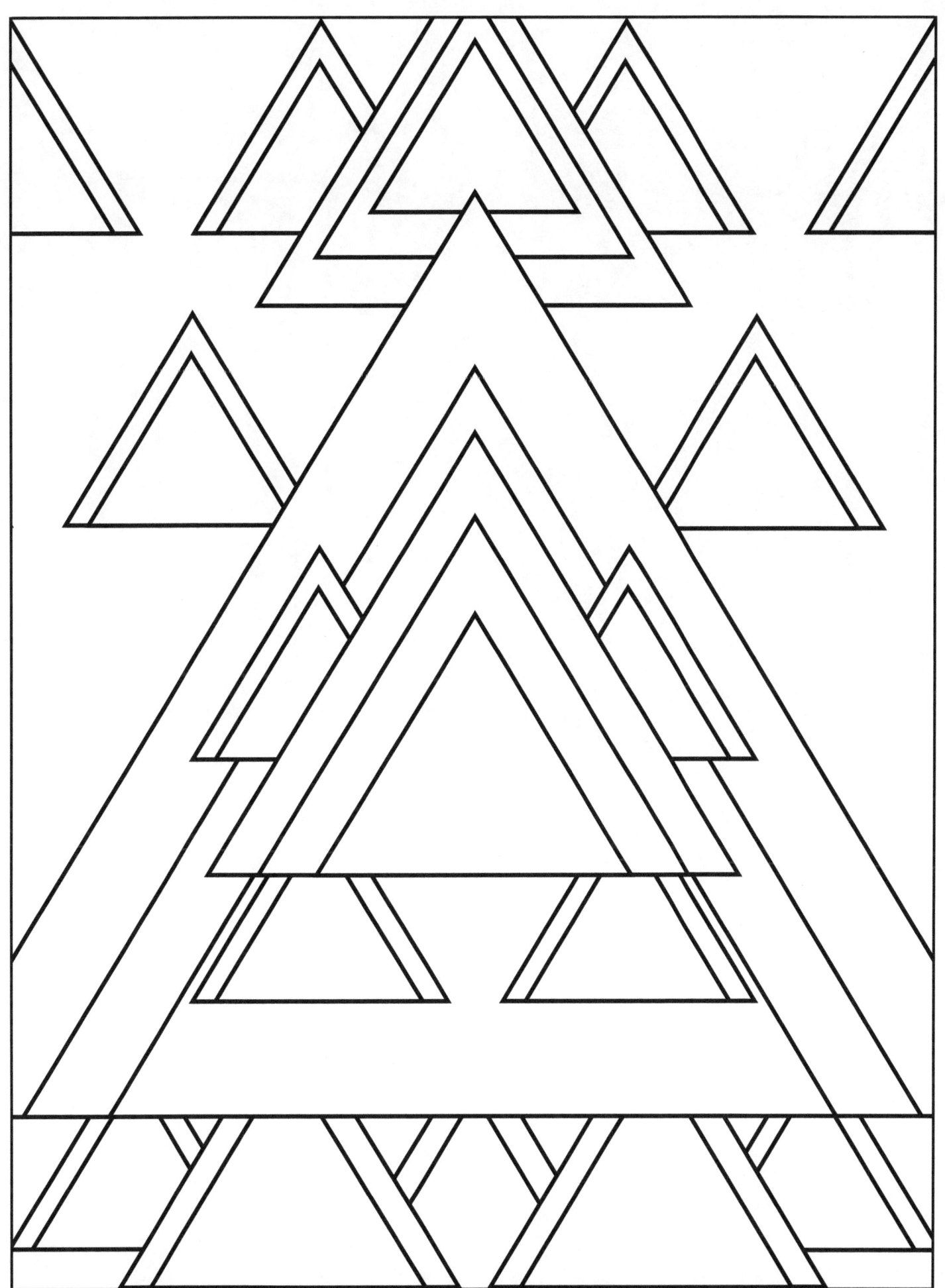

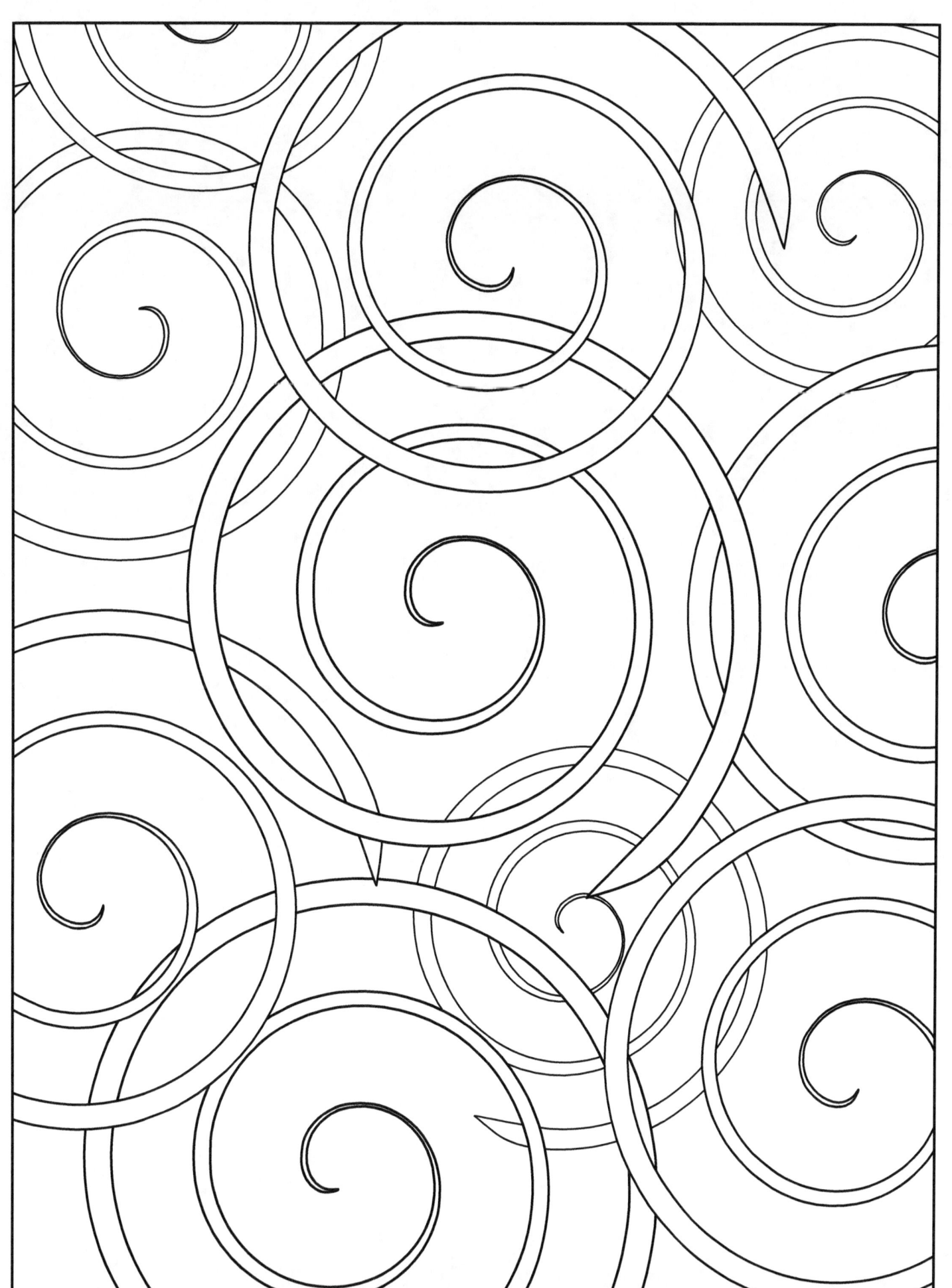

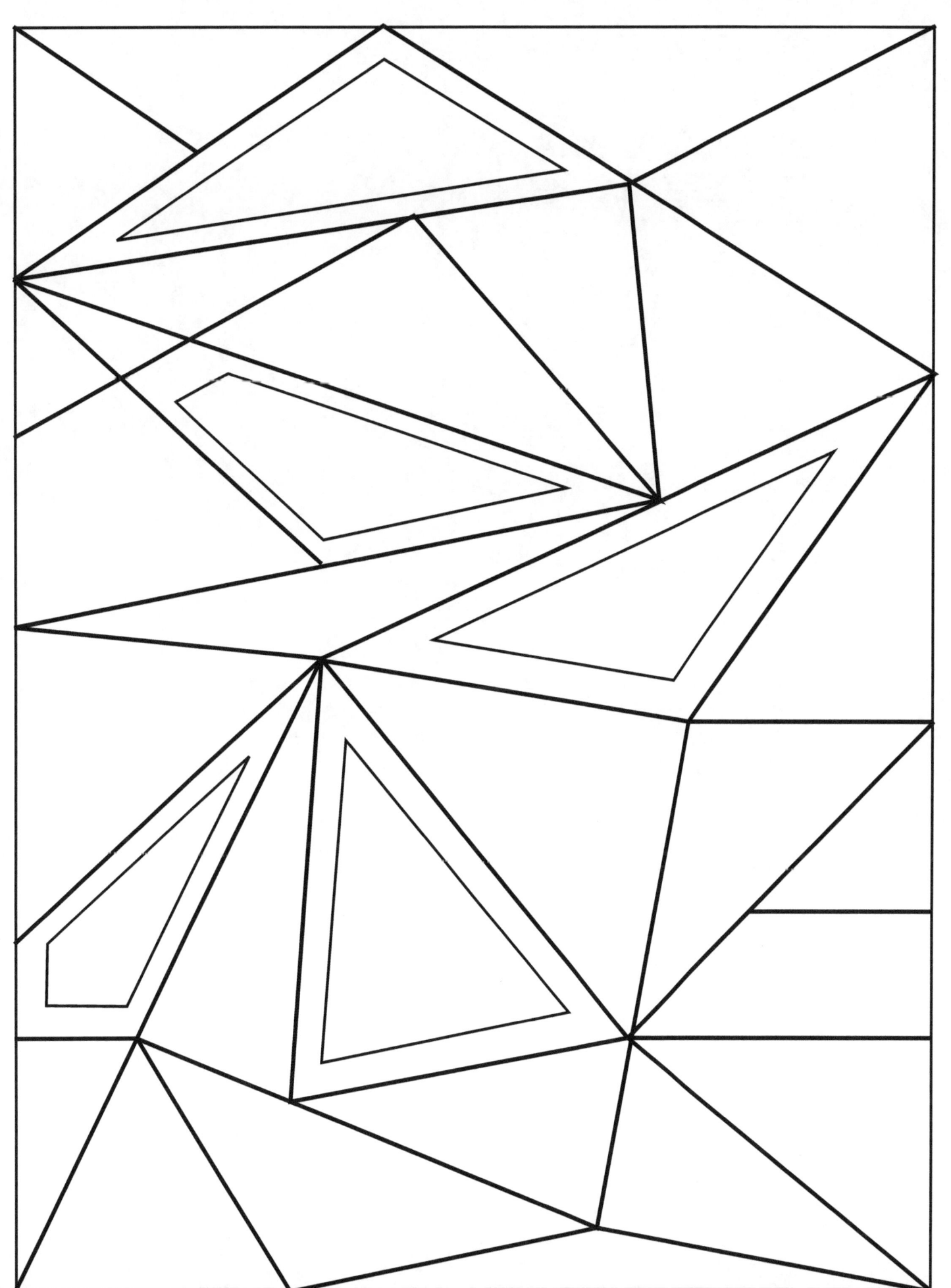

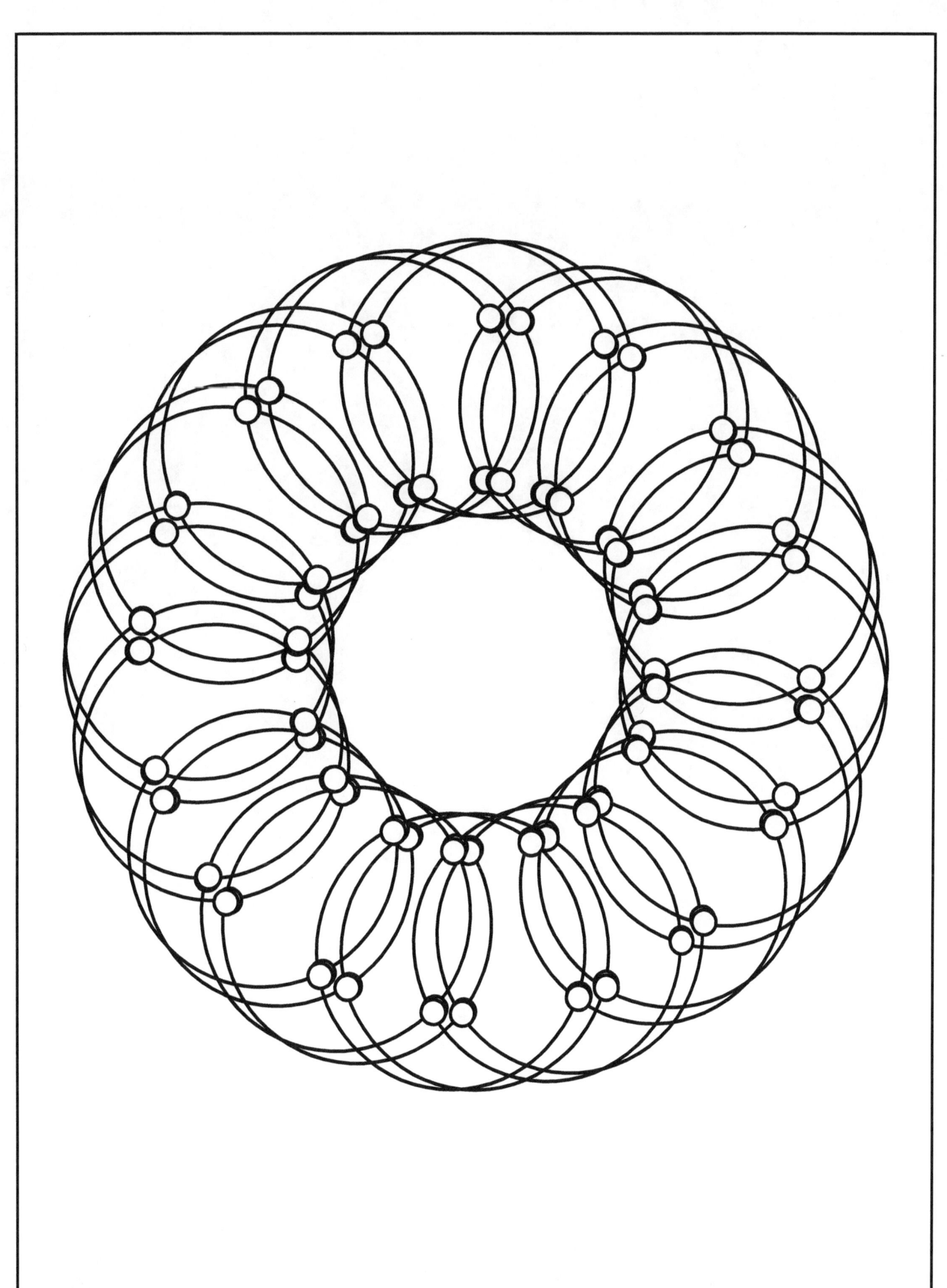

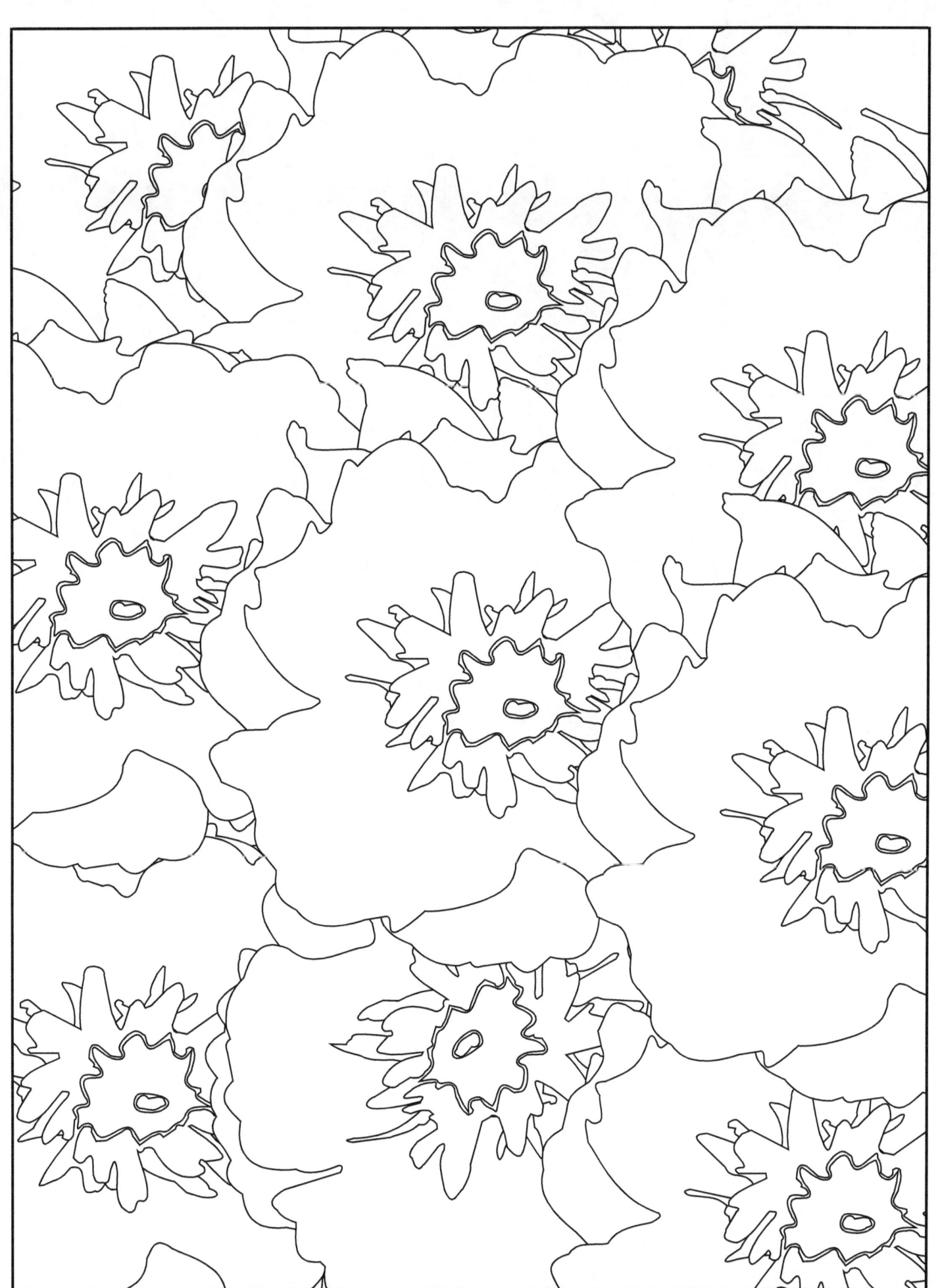

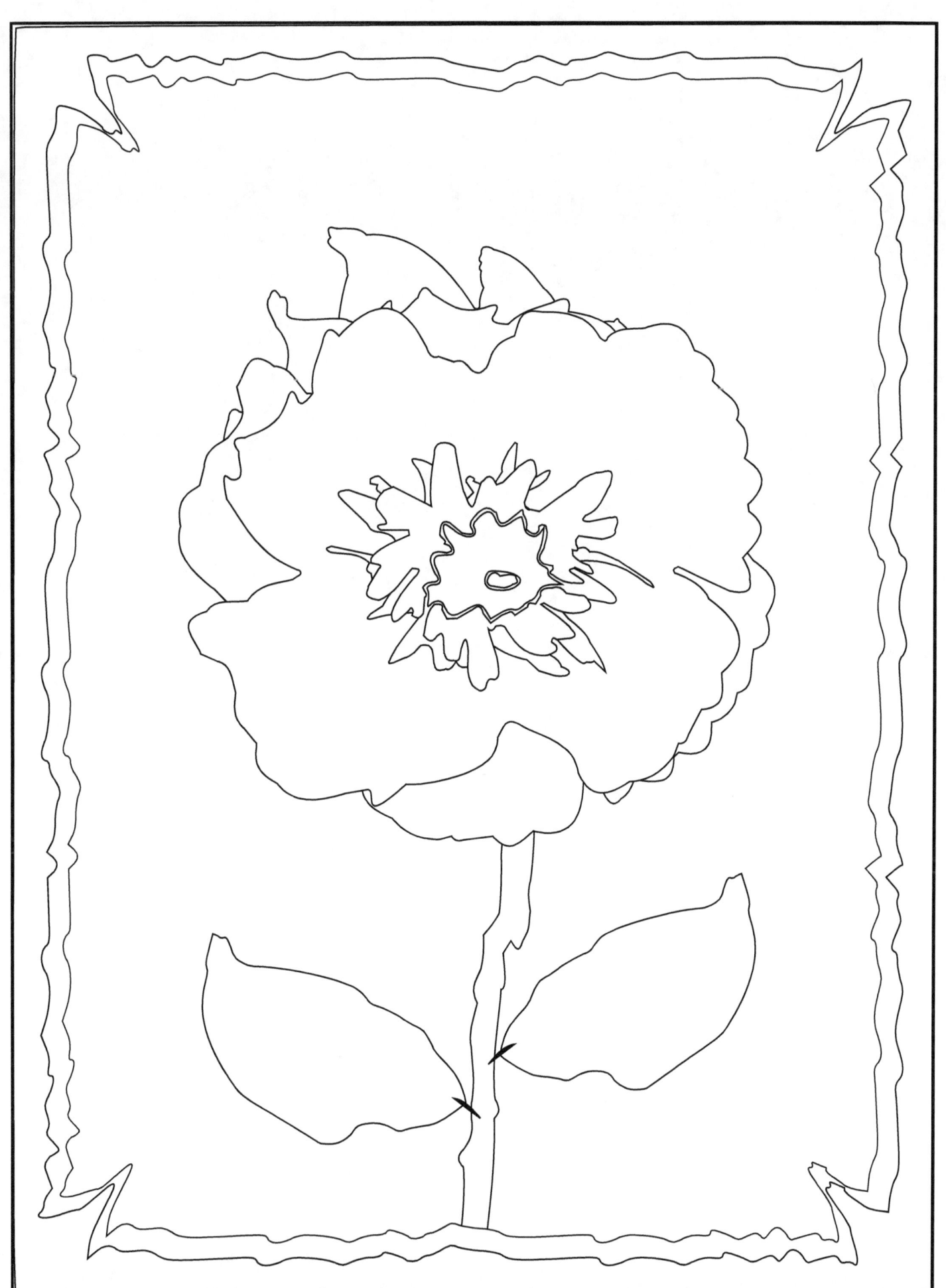

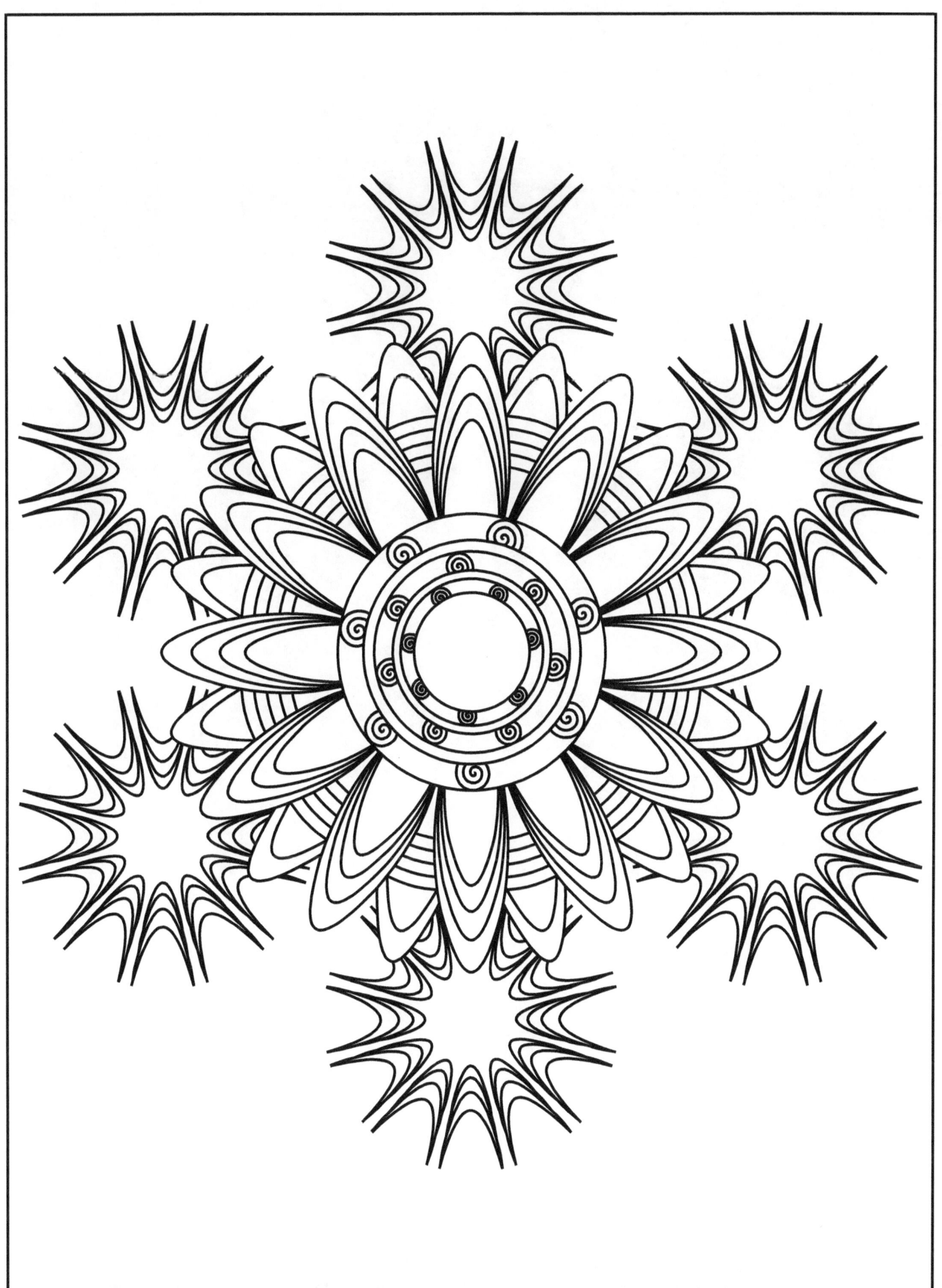

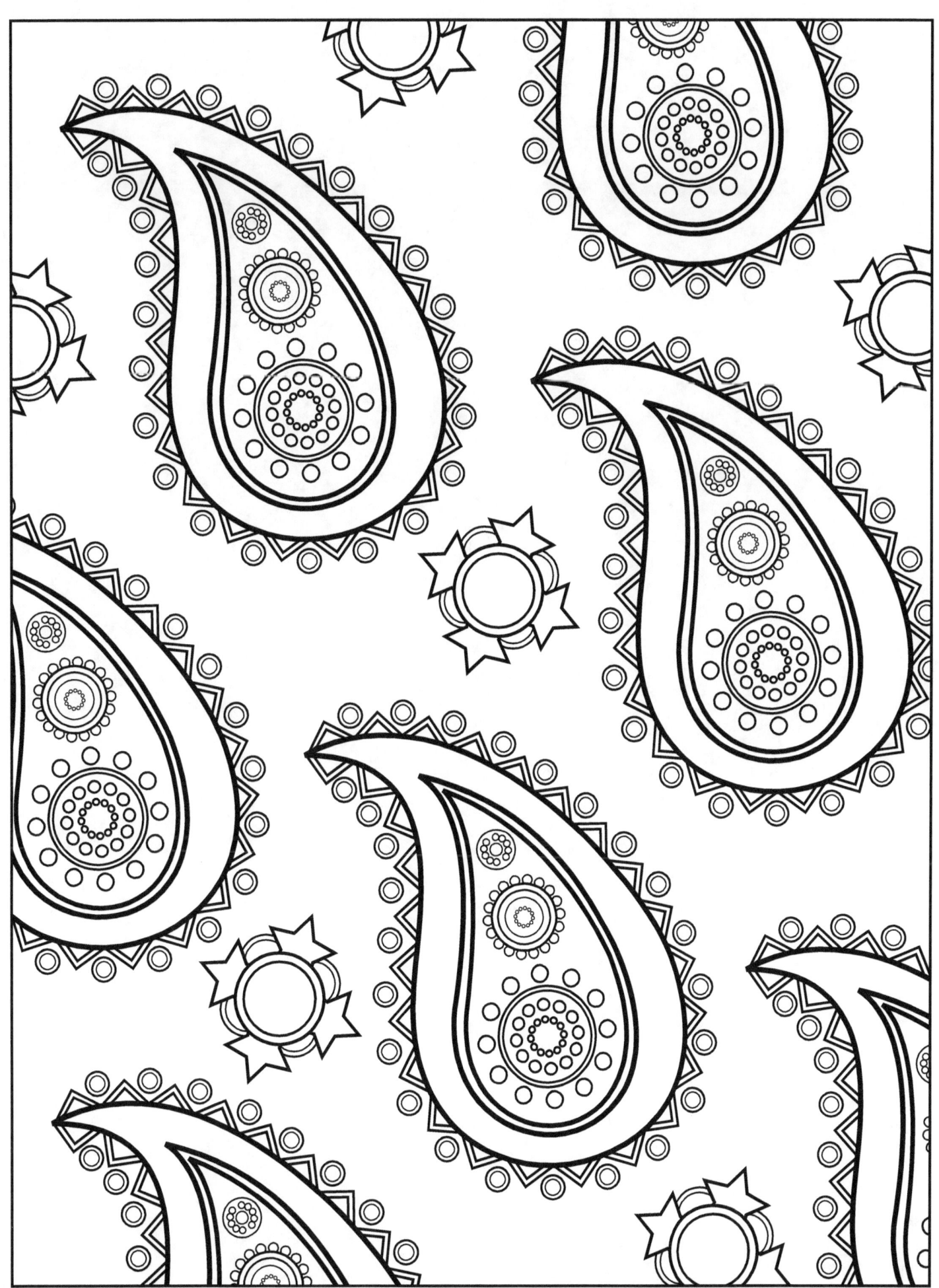

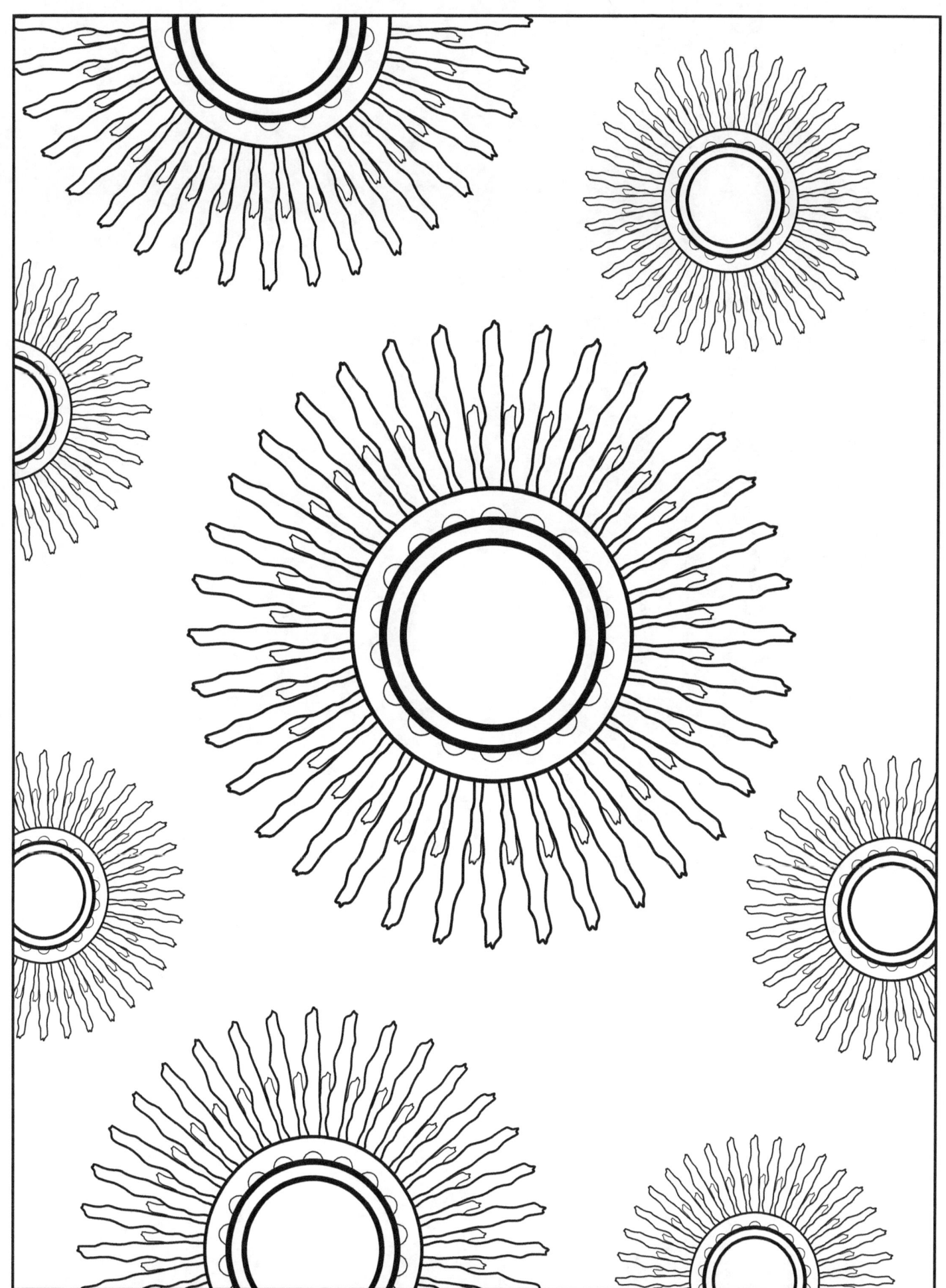

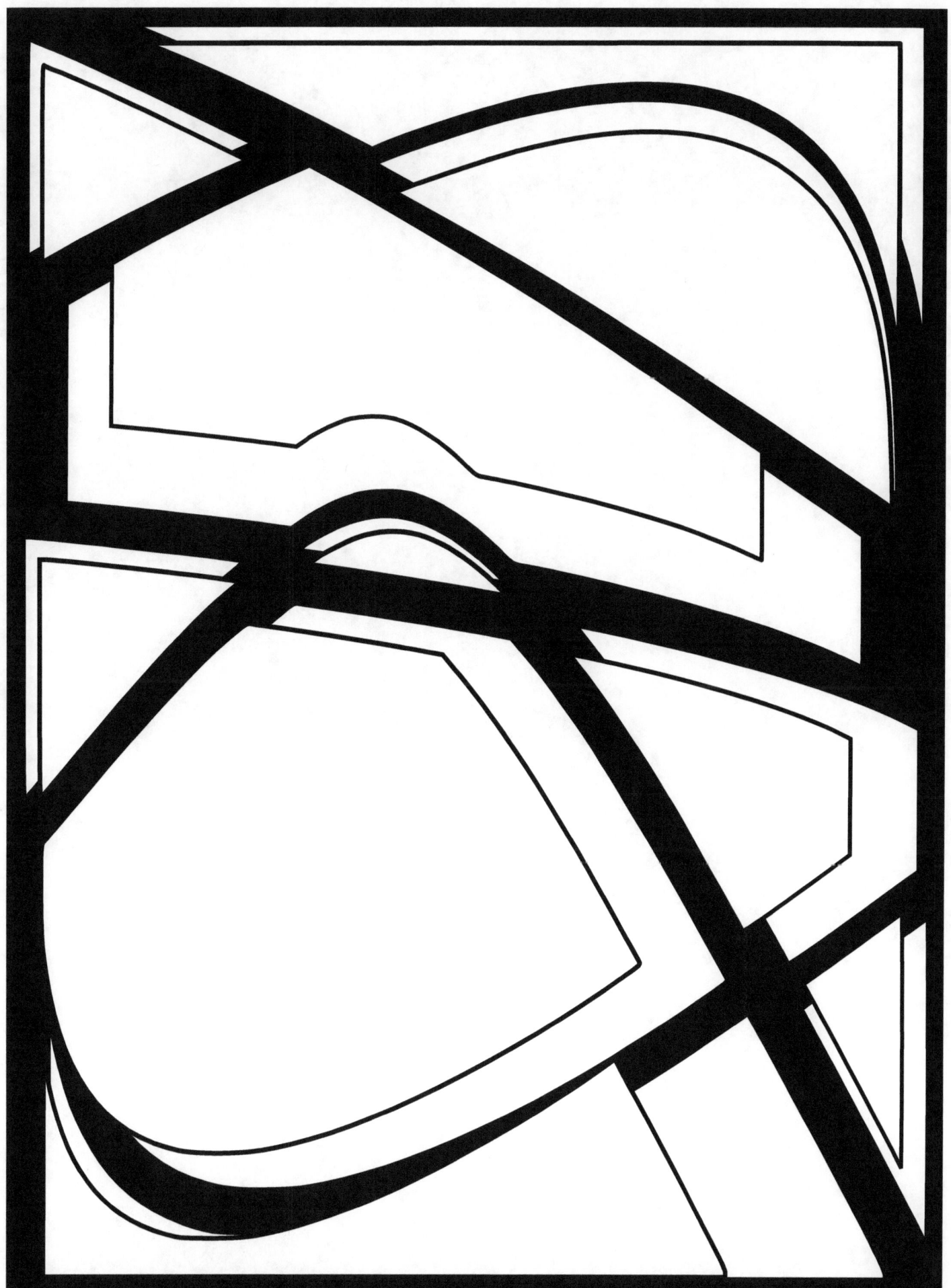

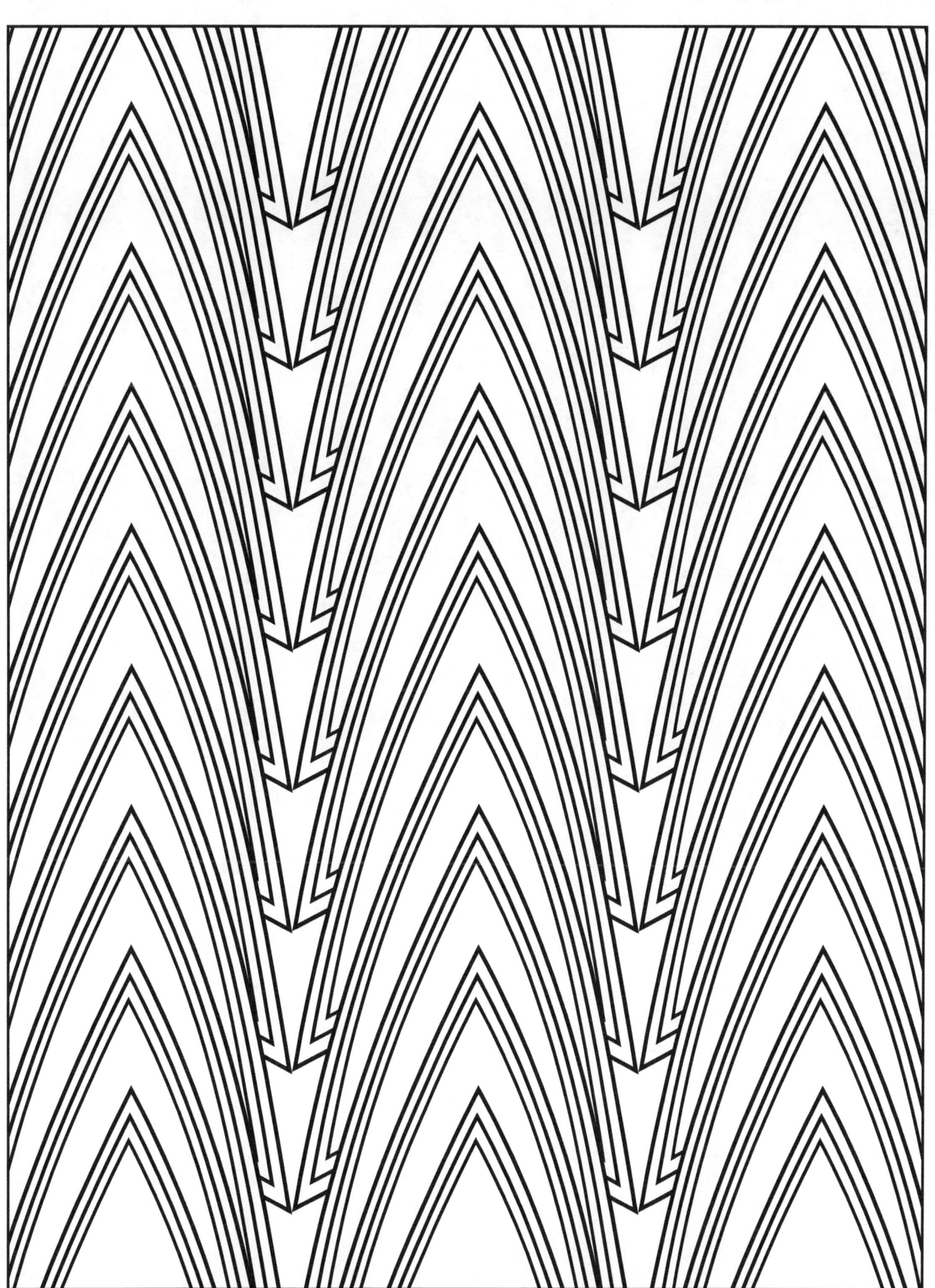